Diversions and Distractions
in
English Literature

Diversions and Distractions in English Literature

R K Bhushan

AUTHORSPRESS
Publishers of Scholarly Books

Worldwide Circulation through Authorspress Global Network
First Published 2011
by
Authorspress
E-35/103, Jawahar Park
Laxmi Nagar, Delhi-110 092
e-mail: authorspress@yahoo.com

Diversions and Distractions in English Literature
ISBN 978-81-7273-567-8

Printed in India at Tarun Offset, Delhi.

With Profound Love,
R K Bhushan.

O Lord SAI,
You alone am!
Lord of Lords,
Deity of Deities,
Invisibly visible,
Inexpressibly expressible,
Animate and the inanimate
as
Movable and the immovable
as
Seeing unseen—
The Prime Mover of All

O Lord!
You are the wire-puller,
Actor of the Universal Stage,
as
Cosmic Reality,
The Supreme Embodiment of Truth,
The Sole Spirit of Existence

—Composed at my request by beloved friend Sai Sudarshan

Preface

To be critical means to be analytical and interpretative to assess and judge the worth or merit, fairly and dispassionately, of the author or the work of art to explore the unexplored in meaning, content, spirit or style. However, the exercise of critical sensibility and faculty means the reflective and poised use of well-informed, instructed and enlightened mind so that it enhances the strength and beauty of art, the artist and the artistic creation. It adds to the delight of the reader and even of the author. The present humble attempt in *Diversions and Distractions in Literary Studies* does not even remotely aim at developing any critical idiom or critical jargon, let alone expounding any critical theory.

The decades of meaningful acquaintance with literary history and literary scholarship, and even clear understanding of the concepts, terms and approaches and attitudes of the innovators and immortals in the genre from the Classicals to the Post-Moderns traversing alive through the Age of Enlightenment, the Age of Reason, Romanticism, the Victorian Age, Modern Age, the Post-War Period, the Post-Modern times and even at present, have their visible influences on my critical sensibility. I owe a deep debt of gratitude to all those Masters in my own studies, understanding, teaching and interpretation of writers and their works from the different periods and literatures.

It is my firm conviction that there can be no criticism without serious reflection and the conscious avoidance of subjectivity. But if this subjectivity comes up with some force in the larger and wider interests of this philosophical activity, it should be welcome, not otherwise. Those who practice this highly skilled and developed faculty come up with something new that sets a trend in this creative activity. Such geniuses fill us with awe and wonder, and stimulate the forces in the field for wider application of their concepts, terms and theories. That is why criticism is an

viii ● Diversions and Distractions in Literary Studies

ever-developing art; it is creation branching out in different directions at different times. So we have a number of approaches, practiced and being practised and still emerging such as Traditional, Formalistic, Psychological, Marxist, Feministic, Cultural (Cultural Materialism & New Historicism), Structuralism and Post-structuralism, Orientalism, etc. There even developed the Criticism of Consciousness, also known as Phenomenological Criticism and Reader-Response Criticism. Obviously, the field has always been rich and fertile.

This is the consistent and unstinted growth of Western Criticism as Creation in the past about 2,500 years. In this context, it is very pertinent to mention that Indian Poetics has also made remarkable advances in Critical Theory and Practice and has also set new directions in the Western Criticism. None can afford to ignore Panini's *Ashtadhyayi*, Patanjali's *Mahabhashya*, Bharatha's *Natyashastra* in this highly significant area of literary and philosophical activity. Secondly, Indian English Criticism has also received fresh impetus and has made its impact felt everywhere, though Indian English Criticism of the British and American authors has also made its mark. We may attribute this phenomenal growth mainly to the creation of new universities and the post-graduate teaching and research in English literatures accompanied by the new proud acquisition of our independent national identity.

In this fast emerging area, given the well-recognized self-assurance, we may mention quite a number of celebrities— P.V. Kane, Suniti Kumar Chatterjee, K.R. Srinivasa Iyengar, S.C. Sen Gupta, V.Y. Kantak, R.C. Sharma, Sarup Singh, A.A. Ansari, O.P. Mathur, A.G. George, C.T. Thomas, B. Rajan, A.N. Dwivedi, M.K. Naik, Shiv K. Kumar, R.W. Desai, K.S. Misra, Chaman Nahal, A.N. Kaul, K.B. Vaid, D.S. Maini, Meenakshi Mukherjee, V. Sachthanandan, Dr. Mohit K. Ray, Kulshrestha...we may continue the list but the limitations imposed by the purpose of this mention. However, it would be unpardonable if I don't mention Aurobindo whose contribution to Literature and Criticism matches the best in the World Literature!

The situation now is so encouraging, the conditions so conducive and also the atmosphere so congenial that not only the professional constraints and compulsions but also personal interests and inspired tastes have created a rising legion of young scholars working overnight to leave new bearings on this genre.

I am a humble camp follower of this legion at the tail with all apprehensions with this book of Critical Essays on a variety of topics dealing with Classical, British, American, Indian English Literature. Some of these essays have been published in reputed international research journals and posted on the websites and I acknowledge respectfully the encouragement I received from them. I am confident that these essays will be of immense benefit to the teachers, scholars and students engaged seriously in post-graduate teaching and learning not only in Indian universities but also abroad. I shall deem myself blessed if these essays succeed honestly in serving their purpose.

R. K. Bhushan

Acknowledgements

My special thanks are to *RE-MARKINGS* and *Indian Journal of Post-Colonial Literatures, Sri-Lankan Guardian*, XX International Poetry Festival at Medellin and other websites for publishing and posting my articles from time to time.

My humble grateful thanks are to Sudarshan Kcherry of Authorspress, New Delhi, who has always been provoking me with new thoughts and ideas to assign new function to intellectuality so that it comes out of its steel frame to serve the entire creation with love and compassion to enlighten. Sai Sudarshan's is a noble soul who excels in what he does and has no pretensions to selfless service. He has made a colossal contribution to my growth and the present status of creativity with profuse Blessings of Sai Baba. I have always been privileged to share his magnanimity more than my due. And he has never grumbled.

Also I am grateful to my great daughters, Sheenam and Geetika, who have ever stood by me to share my learning and leanings   and have shown the courage to rectify my mistakes. My wife, Saroj Sabharwal, and her brothers—Dr. Sudarshan Sehgal, Dr. Surinder Sehgal and Er. Vijay Sehgal—and my son, Vishal Sabharwal, are also deserving of my thankfulness in their own way.

R. K. Bhushan

Contents

1

The Problem of Relocating the Dislocated in Sophocles's Oedipus

The play quintessentialises misfortune; it is an epigram in ill-luck.

— A.J.A. Waldock

Man is dislocated here and all his life's constant and persistent strife is his determined attempt to relocate himself to the place of his ambition and dreams. The entire tenor of this pursuit, relentless or effortless, is decorated with frustration and faith, sureness and success, fall and rise, humiliation and achievement, disgrace and denial. This is always the pre-determined fate of all the high and the low, mighty and the meek, princes and the paupers; and all other millions in mortal form. Who can achieve ataraxy–lauded essential to be happy? Reconciliation born of complete surrender and hard-gained faith alone is the true wisdom needed to fulfil life. All else is futile and fruitless. And when relocation is in sight, we leave with the solace of setting out on our way to relocation. The tragedy of Oedipus, unexcelled in its meaning and amplification and perhaps the richest in drama, ethics, psychology, biology, sociology, philosophy and metaphysics, and even in religion, is the most ideal in history of world drama. The Greek masters and the masses were fully acquainted with the story of King Oedipus but Sophocles's dramatic competence and potentiality have lent to it the status of unchallenged glorious pinnacle.

Oedipus is a world-wonder in his suffering, in his peculiar destiny he is freak. He is a man selected out of millions to undergo this staggering fate; that is why his story is so fascinating. It fascinates because it is so rare; because on any rational assessment his story —

as far as we are concerned—is impossible..... Circumstance has its
practical jokes and its sinister-seeming moods, but a concatenation
of malevolences on this scale is an absolutely unparalleled thing.
(Italics mine)

—*A.J.A. Waldock: Drama of Dramas: The Oedipus Tyrannus*

The very essence of Sophocles's dramaturgy and, for that matter,
its earned greatness, in handling the conspicuous confrontation
between men and gods (whatever be the position of men—only
men, men as men or men higher than their species or men
assuming or equating themselves to be gods)—for that purpose,
gods as destiny (visible or invisible—visible in Oedipus and.
invisible in Antigone and Electra) is definitely to face the reality
of life in a truthfully realistic manner in realization of what human
powers and prowess can be and how far these can be wronged
consciously out of which emerges the realization of the supremacy
of the Highest Order and Harmony and the humility of the highest
temporal authority and will.

Gods must play their game and, that too, on their own terms
and conditions to be imposed and changed as they will, for fun
or frivolity or to make fun of men in their fall or rotting in their
fall. Hounding hands of destiny must bring man to do the evil they
design to trap him into the rationale of the dilemma, as it happens
with Oedipus; any attempt to escape doing evil is also a sin against
gods and have to be penalized in proportion to be judiciously
decided by the gods themselves. According to C. M. Bowra, "*King
Oedipus* shows the humbling of a great and prosperous man by
the gods. This humbling is not deserved; it is not a punishment
for insolence, nor in the last resort is it due to any fault of
judgement or character in the man. The gods display their power
because they will." In "K..ng Oedipus", the Chorus in the 5th Ode
says:

All the generations of mortal man add up to nothing!
Show me the man whose happiness was anything more than
illusion
Followed by illusion.
Here is the instance, here is Oedipus, here is the reason
Why I will call no mortal creature happy.
....
....
Time sees all; and now he has found you, when you least
expected it;

Has found you and judged that marriage-mockery, bride-
groom-son!
This is your elegy:
I wish I had never seen you, offspring of Laius,
Yesterday my morning of light, now my night of endless
darkness! (p. 59)

(Italics in the quote mine)

Destiny dislocates man to carry on the game of the gods who want
unquestioning submission to their known and unknown will.
Man does his best to relocate himself without any sense or burden
of guilt. Oedipus's strife reveals what disasters and damnation
may befall man even in simple quest of simple truth of his
parentage. Destiny further confounded him by answering his
curiosity and the trap was well-patterned and woven till the man
of golden opinions was enmeshed as the foulest and the filthiest
to an unparalleled realization and affliction to be endured till
eternity. Solving one riddle entangled him in other riddles that
redefined his role and responsibility as a redeemer and ruin.
Destiny gave him the illusion of having been relocated to fulfil
his role as a caring and loving king, husband and father only to
be muddled in total shame and the gravest sin. Oedipus, with
cascade descending in scarlet rain from his eyes, says to the
Chorus:

My blood—will they remember what they saw,
And what I came that way to Thebes to do?
Incestuous sin! Breeding where I was bred!
Father, brother, and son; bride, wife, and mother;
Confounded in one monstrous matrimony!
All human filthiness in one crime compounded

(p. 64)

Every infamy, shame and disgrace is the pre-dominant fate that
cleverly and cunningly conspired against Oedipus to this location
by the continuous chiaroscuro of dislocation and relocation to be
located thus! What a play for the festive occasion Sophocles wrote!
And Sophocles doesn't offer any solution; he doesn't even think
remotely of doing so but wants us to accept life and its bare truth
with a sense of unconditional submission to His Will and feel
reconciled. We are marginalized on the boundary lines of life and
must not give ourselves the cause of our suffering and misery.

Pride, simple or human or godly, incenses us to dislocate ourselves from our destination and the aftermath offers to us a picture of dark ruin wrapped in agony and torment. Helpless and enraged man challenges to wait who did it forgetting that we are:

> But helpless pieces of the Game He plays
> Upon this Chequer-board of Nights and Days;
> Hither and thither moves, and checks and slays,
> And one by one back in the closet lays.
>> —*Rubaiyyat of Omar Khayyam*

And also:

> The Moving Finger writes; and, having writ,
> Moves on: nor all your Piety nor Wit
> Shall lure it back to cancel half a Line,
> Nor all your Tears wash out a Word of it.
>> —*Rubaiyyat of Omar Khayyam*

The game of dislocation and callous desertion began with the birth of Oedipus and there was no going back—Citheron, the majestic mountain became the nestling bed of the foster-mother for the infant prince with "riveted ankles". From there again, he was dislocated into the house of Corinthian father, Polybus, and Dorian mother, Merope, till located into the illusion of his parentage. The irresistible curiosity to know the truth of his parentage, he goes to Pythos and returns more nonplussed. The game of dislocation gained further momentum and Oedipus earnestly and honestly made vain attempt to avoid the sin and crime:

> Of horror and misery: how I must marry my mother,
> And become the parent of a misbegotten brood,
> An offence to all mankind-....

And he fled away-putting the stars/ Between me and Corinth, never to see [home again......

The hands of Destiny were hounding Oedipus to guide him to pre-destined dislocations. With whole mind set and determined not to endure the lasting burden of the ever-first sin in the history of mankind, Oedipus wanted to locate himself into a neat, clean and pure life. That is why much is said about the innocence and guilt of Oedipus in the face of the hell-bent malicious gods. The poor Oedipus with all his pre-eminence! The gods are gods and man must not attempt to run away from the ring and let the masters play their bout. Oedipus tells the mother-wife, Jocasta:

> Banished from here, and in my banishment
> Debarred from home and from my fatherland,
> Which I must shun for ever, lest I live
> To make my mother my wife, and kill my father...
> My father...Polybus, to whom I owe my life.
> Can it be any but some monstrous god
> Of evil that has sent this doom upon me

He is cynical about his absolution even. What is lotted cannot be blotted. Rightly said! Time couldn't belie it. How can Oedipus? Albin Lesky says:

> The gods are so very much the more powerful, they shatter human fortune with such deadly certainty, that some scholars have seen nothing else in the play, and have called it a drama of destiny.
>
> —*Albin Lesky*: *Oedipus: An Analytic Tragedy* (p.131)

He says again, "The divine governance, inaccessible to mortal thought, fulfils itself in an appalling manner, but remains always valid and deserving of reverence." (p.131)

It gives to us a psychological convincingness about the supremacy of the gods and the simple moral and social truth is that we, as humans, must not give in or give up. Life is fulfilled only if we make a persistent effort to assure ourselves that we are doing the right and we mean nothing against our creator and preserver, notwithstanding the painful reality of Oedipus that those who attempt to know or scrutinize the unknown, the unknowable and the inscrutable ways of the predominant destiny, howsoever earnest or solemn, must be dislocated so terribly that it becomes an eternal lesson. In all humility, we have to accept whatever be His Will—the only way to be happy! Of course, in His Happiness! We are nobody to exercise the sacred faculty of reason to pass judgement on Him or His Ways. Sophocles' triology of Oedipean plays—*Oedipus Rex, Oedipus at Colonus* and

Antigone-emphasizes the absolute problem of relocating the dislocated. Destiny alone determines what the princes or paupers are to be and what is to become of them.

> Sophocles conceived doomed Oedipus, the greatest sufferer of the Greek stage, as a pattern of nobility, destined to error and misery despite his wisdom, yet exercising a beneficent influence upon his environment in virtue of his boundless grief. The profound poet tells us that a man who is truly noble is incapable of sin; though every law, every natural order, indeed the entire canon of etics, perish by his actions, those very actions will create a circle of higher consequences able to found a new world on the ruins of the old.
>
> —*Friedrich Nietzsche*: *The Birth of Tragedy*; published by Doubleday Company, New York, 1956, p60-61.

After the self-blinding by Oedipus—*What a harvest of ignorance!*— the process of dislocation continues as willed by the Supreme Will. The sons of Oedipus, Eteocles and Polynices:

> ....both slayers, both slain,
> Both stained with brother-blood, dead in a day.....

were tragically relocated in death only leaving behind their sisters, Ismene and Antigone, to face further the wrath of dislocation. Creon, too, can't escape the clutches and claws of the same destiny with his son and wife gone. This triology has an invincible sense of the event the vibrancy of which inspires admiration and reverence in us. E. F.Watling is at his best when he says:

> Oedipus too complacent in his prosperity, too confident of his sufficiency, too ready to take offence or to impute blame when 'rattled' by the approach of trouble; Oedipus unshirking in the performance of a self-appointed unpleasant task, unflinching in quest of the truth at whatever cost of terrible self-revelation; Oedipus driven to the summit of passion by agony of body and soul, and returning at the last to humility and selfless resignation: this vast and living portrait of man, surrounded by a group of subsidiary portraits no less vital, has no equal in the Greek, nor perhaps in any other theatre.
>
> —*Introduction to Sophocles*: *The Theban Plays* (Penguin Classics, Great Britain, 1984).

How Supreme is the Will of God and how unchallengeable and eternal are the laws of the Divine, can be best seen in *Antigone* when Antigone dares King Creon:

> I did not think your edicts strong enough
> To overrule the unwritten unalterable laws
> Of God and heaven, you being only a man.
> They are not of yesterday or to-day, but everlasting,
> Though from where they came from, none can tell.

The Chorus in the 3rd Ode says:

> This law is immutable:
> For mortals greatly to live is greatly to suffer.

The whole house of Labdacus is grueling under the unending burden of tragic dislocations and nothing has helped them relocate themselves—the whole is a story of ruin one after the other till even the whole progeny of Oedipus is dislodged and dislocated with none to scream, none to mourn and none to remember! The Chorus says in the 5th Ode:

> ....So strong is Destiny,
> No wealth, no armoury, no tower,
> No ship that rides the angry sea
> Her mastering hand can stay.

The Messenger also awakens us to the futility of man's strife to relocate himself and to the realization of his humble position in the pre-ordained scheme of things:

> What is the life of man? A thing not fixed
> For
> or evil, fashioned for praise or blame,
> Chance raises a man to the heights, chance casts him
>   down,
> And none can foretell what will be from what is.

Therefore:

> Of happiness the crown
> And chiefest part
> Is wisdom, and to hold
> The gods in awe.
>   —The Chorus in the concluding speech in *Antigone*

Finally, we are left with no other option than to feel the transcending influence in all its serenity and sense of triumph after dealing with this problem in the *Oedipus* plays of Sophocles. We don't experience any frustration or disgust or depressing emotion, though distressed we feel at times and that distress too is elevating. We are not angry at the gods, whoever and whatever they are; we don't find Oedipus guilty or a sinner in all that has happened; and the tragic atmosphere illumines us in and out. From the darkest and the reddest in *Oedipus Rex*, we move on to *Oedipus at Colonus* and experience the blissful calm and tranquility, though the Chorus says:

> Who can say God's purpose falters?
> Time is awake, the Wheel is turning,
> Lifting up and overthrowing.

And the Chorus concludes:

> This is the end of tears:
> No more lament,
> Through all the years,
> Immutable stands this event.

Though "this event" refers to the death of Oedipus at Colonus, yet, I feel, that this speech should have concluded the triology as the story of the curse on the house of Labdacus ends with the end of *Antigone*. The words of Teiresias to Creon come as a final resolution and reconciliation:

> Mark this, my son: all men fall into sin,
> But sinning, he is not for ever lost
> Hapless and helpless, who can make amends
> And has not set his face against repentance.

The problem stands resolved when we feel relocated in our dislocation, in mythology, religion or literature, in complete acceptance of and surrender and submission to His Will and the ungrudging reconciliation that ensues!

Works Cited

Watling, E.F Translated and Edited with Introduction, *Sophocles: The Theban Plays*; published by *Penguin Classics*, Great Britain, 1984.

Luci Berkowitz and Theodore F. Brunner, Translated and Edited, *Oedipus Tyrannus*, W.W. Norton and Company, New York, 1970.

Fitzferald, Edward, Translated and Edited by GF Maine with introduction by Laurence Housman, *Rubaiyat of Omar Khayyam*, Collins, London Ed., 1959.

Hornstein, Percy, Brown, et.al., *The Reader's Companion to World Literature: A Mentor Book*, The New American Library, New York Ed., 1956.

Antigone: A Study in Contrasts of Inexhaustible Dramatic Potentiality

> O Zeus, thou art not subject to sleep or time
> Or age, living for ever in bright Olympus?
> To-morrow and for all time to come,
> As in the past,
> This law is immutable:
> For mortals greatly to live is greatly to suffer.
> —3rd Choral Ode in Sophocles's *Antigone*

Literary judgements are never final. Today, literary approaches change faster than the literary judgements. So no great work of art, especially accepted as a classic, to whatever genre it may belong, can ever be interpreted with any absolute meaning. Some such works are so richly packed with profundities and immensities that they offer interpretive complexities, contraries and contradictions in their historicism, linguism, social and cultural immunism. The aura of the authority of their greatness never diminishes whether the reader is born out of the death of the author or the new author is born out of the creativity of the reader. Their appeal is always sublimating and transcending beyond time and space. Obviously, these creations do not belong to the "literature of exhaustion"; instead, they are "the gems of purest ray serene/ The unfathomed caves of ocean bear." So their luminosity, purity and serenity mock at and defy the latest in critical sensibility and discourse. Sophocles's *Antigone* invariably belongs to this class of literature.

The three plays that dramatize the Oedipodean family history are *King Oedipus, Oedipus at Colonus* and *Antigone*. However, *Antigone* portrays a comparatively simple and single conflict. The heroine, the elder daughter of Sophocles, is a woman of immense intellectuality, abundant conviction and supreme sense of sacrifice for a cause profoundly dear to characters of rare strength. That is the reason that she makes a conscious choice of the coures of confrontation against the authority of the state and the throne whose occupant is her own uncle, Creon. Obviously, Antigone is the champion of feminine assertiveness, unshakable individuality, ennobling dignity and an invincible courage to face hostilities and the spirit never to yield. In this course, she may be broken but not bent. It is in this conflict that the dramatist has woven the complete design to reveal his philosophy of life. The execution is simply marvellous. We know and understand that Creon, the King, could have averted the war between the two brothers and assured a smooth transfer of power in the interests of peace and justice. Then the question of the supremacy of the state authority clashing with the morality of unwritten higher laws would not have risen. Sophocles's vision seems to have had a dimension larger than that. This sets the stage for our discussion of the issue of the contrasts presented and dramatized by the dramatist and the artist and the prophet and the metaphysical philosopher.

More than any other aspect of the play, it is the plenty of contrasts in the action that fascinate us to understand the major concerns and potentialities of this classical tragedy. The contrasts come cascading throughout. The design and the pattern seem to have been consciously conceived and well executed to achieve the desired end. After all, the artist is Sophocles and what else can we expect from him, if not master strokes? E.F.Watling has very aptly said: "This triangular tragedy, of the woman ruled by conscience, the king too confident in his authority, and the young man tormented by conflicting loyalties, it is the function of the Chorus to resolve, gradually, but in the end uncompromisingly, by appeal to God's law, which alone can hold the scales between opposing and imperfect human wills."

As the action of this celebrated tragedy unfolds itself, the contrasts become more conspicuous pointing with sharper and deeper insight to the major issues confronting human beings as they live and face life. Eternally! These are the contrasts of character, relations, purposes; then there are attitudinal contrasts and contrasts of incompatibilities. At the surface level, we see that the play begins with a contrast between the two sisters—Ismene and Antigone. We learn that after the fratricide of two brothers, Etiocles and Polynices, King Creon assumed authority. He has made a state proclamation regarding the cremation of both the brothers. As per the proclamation, Etiocles is to be buried with full state honours for he died a glorious death fighting for the fatherland; Polynices will have no grave, no burial:

> No mourning from anyone; it is forbidden.
> He is to be left unburied, left to be eaten
> By dogs and vultures, a horror for all to see.
> —*Creon in his Proclamation*

Both the brothers are slayers, both slain, and both stained with brother-blood. So one's was the glorious defence of the fatherland and the other's was the inglorious rebellion against it; hence equally ignoble in death. The state declaration has sternly warned its subjects against the transgression of its authority. Determined refusal by Etiocles to go by the mutually agreed terms of ruling the kingdom which led to the bloody confrontation has been completely, and perhaps deliberately, ignored by the new incumbent. And he is considered to be scrupulously conscious of his responsibility to the state. He is also aware of the consequences of its violation—by himself or by any one of the subjects. Creon, being the elderly sire, grandsire, could have intervened and pursuaded Etiocles to honour his commitment and hand over the sceptre to Polynices. It would have largely served the interests of the state and justice. There would have been no open defiance of the state authority and the dictates of the unwritten higher laws of morality. Perhaps deliberately he didn't do so as he could foresee the consequences of such a belligerance—death of both the brothers at each other's hands, leaving behind Creon to be the ruler, his golden dream of his last days. But he could not foresee the determined and obdurate rebellion of Antigone against his authority and the issuance of the State Edict. Also he couldn't foresee the dread of the ruins scattered around him—his son, his wife. The arrogance of being the supreme sovereign blinded him to life around and he saw no sanity or sense in the words of the blind Tieresias. And it has to be and it must be dramatized in the subtle contrasts.

Antigone is an unvanishable symbol of individuality and self-will. She is strongly conscious of her duty to the family honour and sees this proclamation as a discrimination and a humiliating disgrace to the royalty and nobility. We cannot see another motive, may be of occupying the throne, in her rebellion. It was only her familial bonds which emboldened her spirits. Of course, women, even ordinary, show greater courage and endurance in times of such trials. So her individual conscience must revolt against this prevailing situation whatever be the outcome of her revolt and trial. She must defy the destiny and deify the dignity and decency.

She dares the King:

> Justice,
> That dwells with the gods below, knows no such law,
> I did not think your edicts strong enough
> To overrule the unwritten unalterable laws
> Of God and heaven, you being only a man,
> They are not of yesterday or today, but everlasting......

This is a contrast and a clash between individual authority and state authority. Even when the state authority is at war with religious authority, the supremacy of the state remains established whatever be the damage and destruction. Albert Camus has said at some place that a government has no conscience; at the most, it has a policy. Characters like Antigone do not bend. So they must be broken, no matter who else is or are broken and crushed. The dramatic artist in Sophocles must reveal the power and force of the spiritual capacity of man.

Undoubtedly, the direct confrontation between Antigone and Creon is the best and the finest scene of contrast in the play. But it is she who shines everywhere by contrast. She is active, assertive and challenging whereas Ismene is passive, submissive and unchallenging. Ismene is mentally reconciled to accept and live life as it comes to her; Antigone knows that noble death is better than ignoble living. She tells Ismene:

> We have only a little time to please the living,
> But all eternity to love the dead.
> There I shall lie for ever. Live, if you will;
> Live and defy the holiest laws of heaven.

We witness Creon's rage and fury at the hurt vanity of the King. Even the Chorus chides Antigone for being so obdurate and disobedient and audacious. Yes, alone she fights the battle of unwritten laws! Such characters live by themselves, and even for themselves. When the crisis is intensified, they are squarely isolated and deserted. Even the gods desert them, though they establish their victory. The dramatist has revealed her metaphysical inconsolable suffering when she says that she would not have done *the forbidden* for her son or husband. From where to get another brother with mother and father gone? She questions Creon:

> Never a bride, never a mother, unfriended,
> Condemned alive to solitary death,
> What law of heaven have I transgressed?

This is what Antigone willed and that is what the all-powerful blind destiny willed. The Greek tragedy portrays the total helplessness of mortals, be they mighty potentates or paupers or prophets, at the hands of the predominance of destiny. Nothing can change its course or avert its decrees. This is the most happening event in human life where we are left with no choice but to endure His Will. We scream for the fulfilment of our own yearnings only to the mocking laugh of the Supreme governance of life. But who cares except the coming man only to admire and sympathize with such a life as noble and great! We question if it is the meaning of life we humans are to endure; if it is the sole purpose to be achieved for the delight of gods and at this price!

What a grand contrast! C.M. Bowra observes that "more surprising than Sophocles' men are his women. He certainly understood the conventional ideal of womanhood as it was held in Periclean Athens." Are these contrasts the root of all human misery and suffering?

This being the major, there are other levels of contrast— Etiocles and Polynices; Antigone and Ismene; Creon and Haemon; the King and the Chorus; the Prophet and the Potentate; material justice and the divine justice; submission and authority; acceptance and rejection; the respected and the respectable; the antagonist and the protagonist; opinion and judgement; right and right; the noble and the ignoble; the divine assertion and the human assertion; the will and the principles of the Divine governance and the rational choice and the instinctive pursuit of the same; and even between the conception and the execution of this splendid design. These contrasts are so intricately woven in the structural design of the play that it becomes difficult to highlight the one to ignore the other. The playwright's perfect artistry leaves the scholarly reader and the drama critic simply stunned and dumbfounded in his presentation of the end part of the tragedy of the Oedipedian lineage. We come to firmly believe in the Hindu philosophy of the *Karmayoga that we all must, without any exception, reap the harvest of our actions in the life heretofore and hereafter!* Gods do awaken us in their own way and also warn us but we, with our inflated ego or suppressed ego, do not read the writing on the wall. Life continues to evolve and emerge ever by contrasts. The beauty of life is experienced in living through it with all human weakness and strengths to meet the destined will. In life or in death, in shape or in ashes, hopes and aspirations, faith and failures, remain astronomical! What a marvel of eternal significance! Yes, contrasts result in shine and these contrasts rob human beings of their happiness too. Again the inviolable and the inevitable writ of Destiny! Still the humans must show their face to the face of destiny otherwise how shall we realize the sparkling beauty of this living contrast?

We are given to understand in the end that those who disrespect divinity, ridicule prophets and humiliate goodness and disgrace nobility, can't be saved from doom. Happiness comes to those only who learn wisdom through the fear of God. This is an inviolable principle. Heart stricken with pride is afflicted and crushed and pierced with millions of passions steaming out in dark. Alas! We learn the wisdom of life only when we are old and helpless to live the truth of this wisdom. Time alone heals the gashes caused by our unbending self-will and our soul is beleaguered by irrationality closing all doors leading to the realm of spirituality. The Chorus concludes:

Of happiness the crown
And chiefest part
Is wisdom, and to hold
The gods in awe.
This is the law...

Prof. C.M. Bowra has said, "Sophocles peopled his tragic world with superior beings, men of great power and character, women of deep and tender affections. When such fall, their fall is great. The men lose power, reputation, honour, respect, happiness, all that they have desired and enjoyed with their strong tenacious natures; the women lose home, love, contentment, ease, all that has made them happy. In their fall, both men and women may be objects of scorn, misunderstanding and hatred." And the nobility is most misunderstood in the world of human beings. They can't see light at the other end of the tunnel. *This is essentially the essence of being, and, of living too!*

Works Cited

Sophocles: *The Theban Plays* with Translation and Introduction by E.F.Watling, Penguin Edition, 1984.

Bowra,C.M., *Sophoclean Tragedy*, Oxford: The Clarendon Press, 1944.

The Reader's Companion to World Literature—A Mentor Book.

3

The Destiny of Man in Milton with Special Reference to *Paradise Lost*

The teaching and learning of Milton have always been a strenuous exercise for personal as well as extraneous reasons. This has not dimmed or diminished the significance of Milton for the teachers and students of English Language and Literature. And the difficulties experienced by both remain at their own level from time to time, though the main issues and topics of discussion and attempt remain unchanged from the examination point of view. However, now we shall make a departure from the main emphasis, and still, remain within the confines of requirements.

Milton is a poet of very high order, deeply religious with stupendous learning and scholarship, and making an equally devout attempt at reconciling the strains and conflicts in his genius as a poet, theologian and a humanist. Though some men of remarkable critical insight with their spiritual temper have noticed a failure in Milton's promise and performance, his stature remains towering. A poet of astounding immensity and intensity, promise and profundity, vitality and abundance, marvelous scholarship and all-embracive knowledge, Milton is one among the most difficult and formidably challenging poets in the whole range of world poetry. Known for their exuberance and excellence, high-sounding technical perfection, homer, Virgil, Dante, Milton and Aurobindo stand unexcelled and the world, in serious contemplation alone, can hear the *mantra*, the Word and the music divine on Aeolian harp the waves of which keep expanding incessantly. What these waves are measuring and when will the measurement be complete, who knows?

The genius of Milton requires to be viewed in view of the fact that he was born at a time when the dazzling glow of the Golden

Age of English Poetic Drama of the Renaissance had started fading and, by the time, Milton attained his youthful glow, England was in the process of high Reformation in the throes of the challenging political, social and religious turmoil. So Milton had not only to grapple with the moral, spiritual and political crisis in his personal life while playing hide and seek but he had to live through these ignominious times. The more formidable the challenge, the severe the crisis, the more the intellectual potentialities of his poetic genius enlightened the course of this chaotic period and also the chaotic degradation and debasement of the Restoration when all tall promises and declarations proved a hoax. These events have unmistakably and invariably and eloquently reflected and expressed themselves in Milton's poetry and prose asserting the destiny of man as determined by the Divine and as he himself determines it.

Generally, Book 1 of *Paradise Lost* is prescribed for studies at the Postgraduate level. There have been times when the first two books or Books 1 & 4 were there. At the undergraduate level, some sonnet or some significant passage from PL is chosen for the students of English language. What I mean to suggest is that we remain quite ignorant of the major poems of Milton such as *Christ's Nativity Ode, L'Allegro, IL'Penseroso, Lycidas,* and two dozens sonnets, though teachers do refer to *Paradise Regained* and sometimes to *Samson Agonistes* and *Comus* also at the PG level. This is a pity and we are helpless! Very few know Milton as a prose writer—his *Areopagitica, Tracts on Divorce, Education, Marriage,* etc. We observe a strange imbalance in the genius of this greatest English poet, who regarded himself also primarily as a poet that in the standard Columbia Milton, there are 20 volumes out of which only four are poetry volumes. This is another pity. And this is the destiny of Milton here!

When we take up the study of the prescribed First Book of PL, the greatest epic of English Language and one of the greatest in the world literature, we discuss *it's epical features, it's subject and theme, it's grand style, epic similes and, above all, the character of Satan but not Satan as a Character. The little details may lead us to concentrate on the Invocation, the description of Hell, the five speeches of Satan with the Roll Call of the devils and the Pendemonium.* This much honestly done means Milton well introduced!

A strong classical intellectuality mark Milton's poetry. We see "a touch of Virgilian beauty and majesty, a poise of Lucretian grandeur, a note of Aeschylean sublimity, the finest gifts of the ancients coloured or mellowed by richer romantic elements and subtly toned into each other" prepare the Miltonic manner. From his early years, Milton had set his mind on writing a great poem to win the acclaim and admiration of his classical masters and peers. So till he sat to write that poem, Milton had undergone long years of rich experiences of learning, travel, dreams and life which all went into the making of *Adam Unparadized* or *Paradise Lost*. Since it is all related to the destiny of Man here and hereafter, it would be pertinent to have some idea of such a rich background. Milton went on a tour of France, Italy, Sicily and Genoa for one and a half year from early 1638 to August 1639. This is said to have added a new chapter in *the Education of a Poet* and it formed the literary climax of his journey. During this time, Milton crossed the Alps on horseback, went by ship from Nice to Genoa which had long been his spiritual home, through Loghorn and Pisa to Florence for two months, and also met Galileo and other top powers of the time, then to Seina to Rome for two months and then to South to Naples. It may be noted particularly that PL is richly packed and loaded with the images and impressions of this tour. When he returned to England, he was absorbed and lost in barren political controversies and personal and public calamities forced him to return to his poetic powers. In 1651, he became totally blind but was allowed to work with an aid in a separate room till 1655 when there was no option but to retire. Again in spite of political troubles, Milton continued to work for his poetic accomplishment. In 1667, PL was published with little success.

Obviously, PL is not meant for Sunday reading or reading in a church. It is a grand plea by the advocate of life in the Supreme Court of Eternity where the destiny of Man was decided and is decided even today. PL was composed by a blind man, much of it in the sleepless hours of the night. The world of light was replaced by the world of darkness. We are required to have a fair knowledge of the *Bible*, mythology, geography, history, theology, religion, classical literature, astronomy, etc., to understand and appreciate this enduring work of the gifted soul.

Now the main issue.

Milton has stated clearly in the grand and majestic opening of this epical poem that his chief concern is with:

Man's first disobedience, and the fruit
Of that forbidden tree, whose mortal taste
Brought death into the world, and all or woe,
With loss of Eden...

This is the subject/ theme of this enduring work of classical intellectuality. The declared purpose is also stated in the solemn invocation to the Muses. It may be noted specially that the emphasis is on Man, not Satan; and we hear of Satan only in line 34. Therefore the ecstatic soul of the poet bursts out—"Sing heavenly Muse", and the Muse is not localized on Mount Olympian or Mount Helicon as might have been seen by Homer or Virgil but "on the secret top" of Horeb, Sinai so that Milton is led to higher than the "Aonian mount" of classical poets for the subject is higher. Milton is conscious of his blindness—*What in me is dark/ Illumine, what is low raise and support.* Only then, he will assert Eternal Providence and "And justify the ways of God to men." This is how serious the poet is to tell us about the destiny of Man.It may also be noted that Milton has deftly and artistically fused together the three great civilizations which was the main source of Renaissance religious poetry—Classical, Hebrew and Christian.

All artists have and share common concern and depict the same in their own way. That is the destiny of Man—as it is; as it ought to be; as man himself tries/struggles to build it; and the destiny as it turns out to be. Milton's main concern is decidely not the destiny of Satan in spite of the "Satanic School" of criticism. Milton has employed his full poetic genius to reveal the destiny of Adam clubbed with that of Eve. In the beginning, we are highly impressed by the grand, majestic, splendid and luminous Satan who revolted against the Most High. What impresses us about him is Satan as a character but not the character of Satan marked conspicuously by his obdurate pride, ambition, jealousy, disdain and disgust leading to defiance, disobedience, degeneration, degradation, debasement and depravity of which he is tormentingly conscious and even thinks of reconciliation with God when there begins the internal conflict in him. His address to the Sun in Book IV reveals his sense of guilt. He is stung by the consciousness that pride and ambition have cast him down and God deserved no such treatment as he gave to Him. He is in a mood of self-introspection and does so candidly. He even thinks of repentance but his pride reasserts itself and he rejects it as impossible:

> and that word
> Disdain forbids me, and my dread of shame
> Among the spirits beneath.

Since reconciliation is not possible, he is determined to pursue his true nature:

> Evil be thou my Good; by thee at least
> Divided Empire with Heaven's King I hold.

In this context, we may remember his earlier resolve in his second speech in Book I:

> To do aught good never will be our task,
> But ever to do ill our sole delight.

His stubborn will and pride will never allow him to retrace his steps though:

> Under what torments inwardly I groan
> While they adore me on the throne of Hell,
> With Diadem and sceptre high advanc't
> The lower still I fall, only Supreme
> In misery, such joy ambition finds.

Very aptly Prof. C.S.Lewis has said, "From hero to general, from general to politician, from politician to secret service agent, and thence to a thing that peers in at bedroom or bathroom windows, and thence to a toad and finally to a snake—such is the progress of Satan." No doubt, Satan is one of the greatest creations in any language. Heroes rise in their fall and the sight of their fall transcends the audience; they never rise in degeneration and depravity to poisonous detestable entities! How could the noble soul and the blessed personality of Milton sublimate Satan?

The poem was written after a great crisis in Milton's life when his hopes of seeing the Rule of Saints on earth in the Commonwealth had foundered. Since the Fall of Man is the subject, Adam is the central figure, the literary hero on whom is focussed our major attention. Milton's choice of the subject and the choice of the hero at the epic level rouse our wonder and Adam's fall doesn't awaken our admiration for human achievement or grandeur. However, it can't be denied that PL is heroic because of the issues it raises and deals with—the greatness and baseness of man, the noblest virtue and the darkest sins, the clash of Son and Satan. These extremities may grant Milton a legitimate claim that his persons are more heroic than Achilles or Aeneas. So the good in conduct is more important than any other good. By these parameters, we can safely say that Adam's actions and his fate provide unity and the main theme to the epic. It may also be remembered that in Milton's time, Adam was not only a powerful figure in popular imagination but even the Church Fathers also lent him impressive dignity.

Indeed, Adam is the lord of creation; he exists entirely for God and for Eve; he has named animals and they gambol for his delight; his dwelling is decorated richly with the beauty of flowers and trees; lack of splendour in him enhances his natural dignity. Rousseau later imagined him to be the primitive savage of anthropology. He embodies the original splendour of innocence, man as he might have been if sin had not come into the world through the corruption of Satan.

Milton has depicted the life of physical and spiritual bliss in the Garden of Eden as lived by Adam and Eve before the first disobedience. It was a life of devotion, loyalty, faith, purity, understanding, perfect concord, love and beauty amidst the angelic voices singing about them or the bowers where the nightingales sing lullabies to lull them to sleep. In such a blissful state, Adam has two loyalties, both unflinching, to his Maker and to his wife. His thoughts and actions glowed with exalting objects. In his first utterance, he gracefully declares his love for Eve and expresses his gratitude to God for setting him in such bliss. Both Adam and Eve reveal their bliss in their morning hymn, the *Benedicite*, before taking up their daily task. Adam calls on the powers of nature to celebrate their Maker. This is the unfallen state which Adam finds in humble submission to the will of God and doesn't question God's command not to eat the forbidden fruit. When Raphael suggests a danger to it, Adam dismisses it as impossible. Adam is happy to live in the eye of God.

Adam's other devotion is to Eve, the mother of mankind, a superb specimen of female beauty as Adam is of male. Eve is like all young goddesses—like Juno when Jupiter smiles on her, like Flora when Zephyrus breathes on her. And she is only human. And Adam knows it. So is his affection for her and their love is complete, satisfying and unquestioning, spiritual and physical. Milton tells us that their love in this state of innocence is that of an ideal marriage:

Uninterrupted joy, unrivald love.

This love is in sharp contrast with the wanton loves of life today. Since Adam and Eve are to people this earth, they should know each other physically and this knowledge is innocent because God commands and approves it. Until she falls a prey to Satan's temptation, she remains an impeccable ideal of womanhood. We remember how she delights in conversing with Adam and all seasons look charming with him; without him, it is all dull and despairing.

Satan sends a frightening dream to Eve and she finds comfort in Adam. This perfect harmony and union of Adam and Eve excite the jealousy of Satan. Since he knows that he is for ever shut out from such a bliss, he must use every vile and guile to spoil this ideal happiness. So he tempts Eve to taste the forbidden fruit of the Tree of Knowledge and he is successful. Actually it was Beelzebub who suggested to him that he should corrupt Man to afflict agony on God and take revenge. The result is that Adam is completely disturbed but he is torn between two loyalties and makes a wrong choice because his passion for Eve conquers his reason. He can't endure to live without her and must follow her knowing that she is doomed to die, he prefers to die with her—

How can I live without thee, how forgoe
thy sweet converse and love so dearly joyn'd,
To live again in these wilde Woods forlorn?

Once at an after-dinner get-together of the grand masters in the Golden Age of Philosophy in the Intellectual Capital of the world, Athens, love was being discussed as usual. Aristophanes narrated an incident to define love. When there was only one race—Man-

Woman race, God felt a potential threat to His throne from them. The Almighty split the race into two so that man and woman keep yearning to be united all their life and have no thought of invading the heavens. Since then, The throne of the Most High has been secure. Then the question of Will and Choice. All have the will to do and achieve but it is the choice which determines the course of destiny. Once the choice is wrongly made, it is not possible to return and restart. There is an Urdu couplet:

> *Sirf ik kadam utha tha galat rah-e-shauq mein,*
> *Manzil tamam umar mujhe dhoondhati rahi.*

(Only once a step went astray on the path of passion, all life went but no destination was ever in sight!)

Adam yields to his love for Eve and the veil that follows is irreparable. The perfect harmony is broken, marital concord is destroyed, bliss is spoilt and the disaster must follow. Disobedience to god is a fundamental sin for Milton; it is the root of all evil. Adam was forewarned but not forearmed. So his passion conquered his reason and he had no excuse or defence–

> She gave me of the Tree, and I did eate.

The sin of Adam is typical and has psychological significance also. The Tree of Knowledge gives the knowledge of good and evil. They have lost good and found evil; if they had not eaten the fruit, they would have known only good. So they leave Eden covering their shame with pines and cedars and their innumerable boughs. The tragic crisis of the Fall leads to tragic consequences:

> They sate them down to weep, nor only Tears
> Rained at their eyes but high winds worse within
> Began to rise, high Passions, Anger, Hate,
> Mistrust, Suspicion, Discord, and shook sore
> Their inward state of Mind, calm region once
> *And full of Peace, now tost and turbulent. 1X 1121-26*

Adam's love for Eve caused his Fall. It is also the cause of his recovery.

The last two books of PL stress the need for noble, righteous and virtuous conduct in a fallen and disordered world so that man is at ease and peace with himself and the world to escape the feeling of being an absurd in a state of disharmony. Milton offers this new sense and concept of heroism to our attention, to man for his future. This is his reformed heroic outlook, even for our anti-heroes today! So Adam must find his Paradise within. This will rightly determine his rightly chosen destiny failing which disgrace, degradation and degeneration will cause chaos, social, moral, spiritual and psychological. Perhaps we don't have to look far or beyond for living evidence!

Aurobindo says, "Milton has seen Satan and Death and Sin and Hell and Chaos; there is a scriptural greatness in his account of these things. But he has not seen God and heaven and man or the soul embodied in humanity, at once divine and fallen, enslaved to suffering and evil, striving for redemption, yearning for a forfeited bliss and perfection."

All of Milton's poems are, in an important sense, one poem, "the ringing of the changes upon one great theme." It is the theme of the nature and the destiny of man—of knowledge and self-knowledge—of the peculiarly human predicament in which man experiences alienation and yet must strive for wholeness. So:

Tomorrow to fresh woods and pastures new.

Works Cited

Crehan, T., Edited with a critical commentary, *Paradise Lost Books, I and II*, New Delhi: B.I. Publications, 1975.

Lewis, C.S., *A Preface to Paradise Lost*, London: Oxford University Press, 1967.

Bowra, C.M., *From Virgil to Milton*, PAPERMACS, Macmillan & Co Ltd. Oxford, 1944.

Aurobindo, Sri, *The Future of Poetry*, Pondicherry: Sri Aurobindo Ashram, 1994.

Nicolson, Marjorie Hope, *A Reader's Guide to John Milton*, London: Thames and Hudson Ltd, 1970.

Elledge, Scott (edited), *Paradise Lost, John Milton; A Norton Critical Edition*, U.S.A., Second Edition.

4

Celebrities in the Poetry of Ted Hughes—
The Civilisation beyond the Civilisation

> You will know best of all if you go to the market, and see
> whole yard-lengths of robins, like coral and onyx necklaces,
> and strings of bull-finches, goldfinches, larks, sparrows,
> nightingales, starlings, temptingly offered along with
> strings of sausages, these last looking like the strings of
> pearls in the show. If one bought the birds to wear as
> ornaments, barbaric necklaces, it would be more
> conceivable.
>
> —D.H. Lawrence in *Man is a Hunter*

Every song written by a poet is a celebration of the mood and the
moment, sight and soul, sanctity of love and life with all their
simplicity, sorrow, stupidity, sagacity and sublimity. It may be a
song of Nature with the rich variety and richer harmony and
balance of its inhabitants, in smart comparison or sharp contrast
with that of the Crowning Creation of the Supreme. This faith and
truthfulness of the artist in poet alone is the eternal treasure of
poetry everywhere. To this truthfulness and faith, Ted Hughes
lends new force and splendor when he portrays animals, birds
and beasts and finds them greater than man. That is why he
admires and idolizes them and they—Wodwo, hawk, jaguar, fox,
otter, pike, crow, thrushes, tomcat etc.—become Ted Hughes's
celebrities, and the whole kingdom of Nature dipped deep in the
poet's philosophy of life and life force comes alive. The force and
ferocity, strength and speed, violence and virility of the imagery
and rhythm used, mostly consciously in his poetry have gained
artistic compatibility with his beasts, animals and birds. Their
intellectual discipline with their violence and vigor hold some
special appeal. Charles Tomlinson has said, " Hughes has what

few English poets of his time possess—a sense of nature, a sense of that other England which the London-bound writer has forgotten....His animal poetry (see his evocations of otter and pike) is excellent, and he brings to animal subjects, and sometimes to landscape, a feeling for their stark impingement far beyond the range of any of his *contemporaries...potentially the most powerful and fertile poet in the last twenty years.*" (From his essay on Ted Hughes in *Pelican Guide to Modern Age*)

Ted Hughes's absorbing interest in the civilization of animals provokes our abundant interest. The magnificence, dexterity, ferocity, vitality, violence, strength, dare, speed and smart movements of the animals and birds, and even their endearing and lovable violent conduct, fill the poetic landscape of Ted with queer wonder and admiration for nature, and he is disgusted and embittered how man, instead of improving himself towards sublimation, is ever-ready to destroy this world. In one of his interviews, he boldly wished that man, instead of developing his intellect in the evolutionary process, should have developed his third leg since these birds and animals live better and in greater harmony without intellect. Even pre-lapsarian man could not stoop down to this level notwithstanding his fierce struggle for existence. Man's relentless mad ventures to denude and devastate their habitat have failed to disturb their harmony and balance, though he has disturbed his own ecological balance beyond repair. Ted Hughes is deeply pained and anguished at this mess and he eloquently expresses the same in heaping lavish adulations on this kingdom nowhere near the kingdom of this ruler of the world.

Shelley's myth-making imagination is unexcelled and superb for he has humanized the objects of nature and created lasting beauty and splendour in English poetry. Similarly, Ted Hughes has vested animals, beasts and birds with the qualities and virtues we trace in man, though man is the borrower, partially or wholly, of all these personality traits from their planet of purity, harmony and balance and truthfulness with no hidden agenda. "He often comments on the human condition through the use of myth and symbol, describing natural phenomena and animals in evocative language. Hughes contends that the western civilization has overhauled intellectual faculties, dividing humans both from their instinctual urges and from nature." (From *Introduction to Contemporary Literary Criticism*, Hughes, Ted (Vol. 119).

Ted awakens us to his re-invention and innovative use of myth and legend and he redefines the use of language to lay bare human folly in causing destruction just for delight. The poet is an essential eco-critic in whose visionary quest and pursuit, we clearly trace his ecological value system. He seems to be a sage with keen observation watching the animals and birds in the aviary and zoo of nature. It may not be wrong to say that he leads us into the civilization beyond the civilization. Thus this twentieth century giant, inventive and innovative poet charged into the domain of dominant trends in the poetry of the second half of the twentieth century. In a strikingly suggestive manner, Ted Hughes redefines the role of the poet as a potent source of reuniting and reunifying the wide apart Man and Nature by redirecting his emotional and rational energies.

Ted's dramatic emergence on the world of poetry in times of crisis and then the disappearance of the British Poet-Laureate on October.28, 1998 created a yawning gulf in English poetries though this world is amazingly populated today. The day he was noticed in the loosely-organized assemblage of poets, the so-called "Group", he never looked back and it was a turning point in his career. This 'Group' performed the function of the formative critical workshop where the atmosphere of watchful sobriety, rigors of unsparing criticism and, of course, mutual esteem and emulation prevailed, met in Cambridge under the Chairmanship of Philip Hobsbaum and then once a week at the house of Edward-Lucie Smith in London to discuss one another's poems. Among others who were in this 'Group' were Peter Porter, George Macbeth, Peter Redgrove, Alan Brown-John and Martin Bell. It was in this 'community of letters' that Ted Hughes came to light in the mid-1950s even before the publication of his *The Hawk in the Rain*. Charles Tomlinson found him "easily the most interesting of the younger poets" and A. Alvarez described him as "a poet of the first importance." That was perhaps the time when fertile grounds were broken for the civilization beyond the civilization.

What makes Ted Hughes the most interesting poet of the first importance is obviously his well-studied and well-observed and seriously well-reflected physiognomical and psychological, even cultural and aesthetic, built-up of animals, beasts and birds. It is beyond doubt, with a negligible margin of doubt that Ted Hughes stands in a class by himself in this respect. Spenser is rightly the Poet's Poet or the New Poet; Milton is the greatest poet of our English language; Dryden and Pope mirror the society in their own neo-classical way; the nineteenth centuryd. Romantics carry the stamp of their deep-rooted individualism expressed in strong emotionality by adding new charm to the love of the distant; Tennyson and Browning were potential spokesmen poets of the Victorian Age, though the hidden spirit of melancholy was captured by Matthew Arnold, Fitzgerald and A.H. Clough in the colour-blooms of passion and sensuality of the Pre-Raphaelites broadening the further lanes, by-lanes and courses for the moderns and post-moderns among whom we may say T.S. Eliot dissected the stinking malady of our civilization; Yeats went on to be personal, political, social, historical and mythological in his matchless poetic potentiality. However, the post-Second World War scenario added new dimensions to the poetic process, and Ted Hughes made a conspicuous departure from the mood of the times and out of his bold initiatives in themes and techniques emerged a new civilization not even remotely akin to our own civilization. So Ted Hughes enjoys a taller and more dignified stature beside his great contemporaries like Auden, Larkin, Hopkins, R. S. Thomas, Thom Gunn, etc. That is what lends fascination to the poetry of Ted Hughes.

In the light of these observations, it is more than important to know what experiences, observations and influences and inspiration shaped and moulded the poetic sensibilities of Ted Hughes. It may be noted at the outset that his humble beginnings and humble employment never humbled the artist in Ted Hughes. His mind was shaped and carved and his over-all personality was deeply influenced by a variety of experiences and irresistible fascinations in everyday life. Most notable among them were his father's experiences in the First World War, his angler, hunter and game-keeper brother, his close interaction with the miners, railway men's children, woods and lakes, his employment as a wireless mechanic in the RAF, gardener and a watchman, even his stifling academic pursuits at Cambridge, initially of English Literature but subsequently shifting to anthropology and archaeology and his great fascination for F.R. Leavis whose lectures he would attend attentively and affectionately. Thus his philosophy of life was well-evolved, his poetic activity and creativity had decided a chosen course. Lawrentian sympathies inspired in him the deep-rooted love for the strength and vitality as essential and indispensable for survival in this hostile and inimical world; so was born his love for beasts and animals. It would be a grave error if we overlook Ted's voracious craze for reading Shakespeare and his marriage with the American poetess, Sylvia Plath, with whom it became a legendary couple and this contributed to Ted's poetic growth and accomplishment. On his return from America, Ted found that his first volume of poems, *The Hawk in the Rain,* had become the choice of Poetry Book Society and came out triumphant from the rigours of criticism. This is how the poet was not only made but was also widely accepted.

The sensitive soul of the artist has always rued and lamented the ruthless and willful devastation caused by man to the world of Nature as a whole. Of course, no person can remain indifferent to the naked show of cruelty, malice and atrocity solely for delight. There are some who react and respond more eloquently and lamentably to the sorry mess created by man's continuous and vigorous degradation of the most splendid and richly precious heritage—the harmonious and blessed Kingdom of Nature, created in the image of Heaven, and that of animals. Both are now faced with severe threat of extinction. D. H. Lawrence's "Nature and Poetical Pieces", the First Section of the Part One of *Phoenix,* is a living record of the sounds and harmonies, brilliant hues and shades and sights of the lavish blessings of Nature and its inhabitants. Such artists have shown their deep concern and anguish, and even it mounts to be a crushing indictment, at what man has done and is doing to this blessed kingdom. Ted Hughes has the same strain running in him and he has expressed it in his own language and diction, called "orghast" or "talking without words"—the chief strength and the striking feature of his poetry. J. A. Stone says, "He sees power and vitality as essential principles always contending against death, to failure of God to create a satisfactory universe, the ever-present strength of evil, and personal survival as the only goal to achieve....In animals, he sees the certainties, the pointlessness, and the violence that are part of man's life, and he uses them to clarify and intensify human experience." This observation is a powerful pointer to major focus and emphasis in the poetry of Ted Hughes.

Here the two civilizations not only stand apart in tall contrast but also establish the clear preference of the poet. He looks beyond the high walls of human civilization and doesn't find any disquiet, restiveness, frustration, nervousness, paralytic heart or head, artificiality or superficiality, deceptive dazzle or glitter, no man-made system of governance and justice, no propaganda or malicious campaign, no bloody course to power or overthrow to usurp, no unscrupulous practices to wean away man from man. This is a civilization of peace and purity assured by the laws of divine governance. Well envisioned, Ted! A sample analysis of some of his most anthologized and most popular and more than the most quoted poems shall substantiate and authenticate the present studies or thesis.

The openings of the poems of Ted are striking; they open with the dramatic strength and speed and violence of diction and rhythm. This does take us to the seventeenth century School of Metaphysical Poetry though the thought-content of these poems is entirely different. For instance:

> Now is the globe shrunk tight
> Round the mouse's dulled wintering heart.
>
> —"Snowdrop"

Or

> Comes home dull with coal-dust deliberately
> To grime the sink and foul towels and let her
> Learn with scrubbing brush and scrubbing beard
> The stubborn character of money.
>
> —"Her Husband"

Or

> "A cool small evening shrunk to a dog bark and the clank
> of a bucket"
>
> —"Full Moon and Little Frieda"

Or

> Burning
>   burning
>   burning
>   there was finally something
> The sun could not burn,..
>
> —"Crow's Last Stand"

Or

Bones is a crazy pony.
Moon-white-star-mad,
All skull and skeleton.

—"Bones"

Or

I climbed through woods in the hour-before-dawn dark.
Evil air, a frost-making stillness.   —"The Horses"

Or

Terrifying are the attent sleek thrushes on the lawn,
More coiled steel than living—a poised
Dark deadly eye,...   —"Thrushes"

Or

At nightfall, as the sea darkens,
A depth darkness thickens, mustering from the gulfs and
the submarine badlands.   —"Ghost Crabs"

Even the openings of the poems of Ted Hughes immediately
transport us far away from the human life and man's far-advanced
civilization into another world, the world of nature, the world of
beasts, birds and animals—so fascinatingly and passionately, and
so affectionately portrayed by the poet in the original language
used by the inhabitants of that civilization. This civilization comes
alive in its fullness in "Crow and the Birds"; the poem is a bird
sanctuary wherein we hear no sounds and voices of the birds but
we witness a stunning variety of birds busy in their own dexterous
way. Ted's observation and presentation have nothing to do with
emotion or sentiment; it is a world of birds in reality, the world
of flights in its full view; it is a harmonious mix of their culture
and civilization. In fact, this is the crux of the dynamics of his
philosophy of civilization, perhaps a hard-boiled realization. A
bird-watcher Ted Hughes tells us about the soaring eagle,
trawling curlew, swooping swallow, sailing owl:

And the bluetit zipped clear of lace panties
And the woodpecker drummed clear of the rotovator
and the rose-farm
and the peewit tumbled clear of the laundromat....

while the bullfinch plumped and the goldfinch bulbed, the wryneck crooked, the dipper peered and, last of all:

Crow spraddled head-down in the beach-garbage, guzzling
a Dropped ice-cream.

Do we remember we are in man's civilization? Does it not throw us into oblivion to lead us in the thick of civilization beyond civilization?

This civilization is born out of Ted's admiration, fascination and idolization of animals, birds and fishes and it captures our immediate attention and deserves our special consideration. He intellectualizes their physiognomy, activities, habits, their potentiality and dexterity to survive under hostile conditions and their inborn capability to be in harmony with the environment without being exercised or stressed with any fear or danger from the delight in killing. Ted is aware of the dead potency of man in this barren civilization. He is a manly poet who touches upon manly subjects with manly skill in a manly manner to convey his manly message. His main thesis is that man has lost the vitality and strength leading him to the barrenness and sterility of civilization. That is why Ted Hughes uses suggestive, forceful, assaulting, violent and ferocious language and diction and evocative images. His metaphors are not only bold but abundant also; they fall like hammer-strokes to scare us into the meaning. *The Hawk in the Rain* (1957) and *Lupercal* (1960), according to Anthony Thwaite, "concentrated on physical vividness of a mimetic sort, in a turbulent world of predatory animals, primitive violence, and moments of extreme human endurance—a bloody world ruled by impulse and instinct" with:

No indolent procrastinations and no yawning stares
No sighs or head-scratchings.

—"Thrushes"

Ted Hughes makes a persistent and consistent convincing effort to prove his conviction in poem after poem and even in his interviews and letters. After we are acquainted with his instinctive and intuitive love with his vital intellectual passion, we are intently watching the denizens of his civilization at play in their activity or inactivity. His *Wodwo*, which became the title of his 1967 collection of poems is an invariable image of the poet's interior and exterior landscape of the civilization that in fact is a civilization which needs no emancipation from the serious maladies of tensions that paralyze our heart and head; where there is light in darkness; where there is no rancour, no bitterness, no burning jealousies and no killing envies; no evil eyes or looks to destroy or torment the fellow denizens. To be concise:

There is no hidden agenda in the stagnant progress of this civilisation and its denizens hold out a powerful and loud message to man's impotent will to drag himself into the material mud and slime.

Ted Hughes gives a formal introduction to *Wodwo*, fully deserving to be idolized, in his "Poetry in the making" *as*: "Here is another poem of my own about some sort of goblin creature— I imagine this creature just discovering that it is alive in the world. It is quite bewildered to know what is going on (*underlining mine*). It has a whole string of thoughts, but at the centre of all of them as you will see, in this creature and its bewilderment. The poem is called 'Wodwo'. A Wodwo is a sort of half-man half-animal spirit of the forests. Throughout the poem, Wodwo is frantically confronted with the dilemma of tracing his identity and relationship with the surrounding and its creatures. Wodwo is irresolute and indecisive like Hamlet. However, Wodwo is neither insane nor pretends to be so. It is a poem of deep psychological, physiognomical and sociological introspection in which Wodwo, half-animal, half-spirit, seriously reflects on his positioning in the hierarchy of relationships in the pattern of existence. Wodwo has been portrayed as a character which fails to define itself as it is non-plussed at what is happening around. *Wow Ted!* However, his process of discovering his real and exact self and identity is unending as Wodwo questions:

Who am I?................
....
What am I to split.............
....
What am I doing here in midair?
....
do I fit in their world?
....

—"Thrushes"

The questions continue to crop up in the mind of Wodwo but remain unanswered. We are faced with the fury of the flood irresistible in the cultural, aesthetic and intellectual fusions and confusions, so spontaneous in force revealing Ted's fascination with equal spontaneity and force. His artistry is astonishing in unique stylistic flow of the subject and the spirit. On the bosom of this poetic technique employed by him is a pointer to the rootlessness and no belongingness of Wodwo who says:

> ...I suppose I am the exact centre
> but there's all this what is its roots
> roots roots roots and here's the water
> again very queer but I'll go on looking.

> —"Wodwo"

At one point, Hughes came out with a stinging onslaught on man suggesting that man, instead of developing his intellect should have developed his third leg and animals, beasts and birds are better-off without intellect. He obviously jeers at the man on the pyramids of civilization who is engaged in the debasing occupations. He says:

> With man, it is otherwise. Heroisms on horseback.
> Outstripping the desk-diary at a broad desk.

> —"Thrushes"

Ted's frequent use of half-sentences lends new vigour, movement and picturesqueness to his innovative poetic style and themes. In his conscious attempt to intellectualize, the poet appears to be unsentimental. "The Jaguar" is a fine example; it is a poem of movement, force, ferocity and velocity. The jaguar mesmerizes the crowd that watches him in the cage. And he watches them in all his majesty. The poetic idiom, metaphor and technique employed by Ted to acquaint us with the jaguar, the largest animal of a cat family, are equally assaulting like the shots of a gun:

> a jaguar hurrying enraged
> Through prison darkness after the drills of his eyes.

> Or

> a short fierce fuse,
> the bang of blood in the brain deaf the ear.

> —"The Jaguar"

This leads us to a glorious climax:

> His stride is wilderness of freedom:
> The world rolls under the long thrust of his heel.
> Over the cage floor the horizons come.
>
> — "The Jaguar"

This is the poet's innovative way of connecting images with thoughts. When we clearly visualize the undeified and undefiled nature, we question ourselves if the crumpled and balled will of man can be a match with Ted's idols. "Fatigued with indolence", "Lie still as the sun", "The boa-constrictor's coil" and much more in the language of the civilization created, not portrayed by Ted Hughes:

> It might be painted on a nursery wall

Or we may paint it on the wall of our living room to feel the living presence of the very source of our origin and the true fountainhead of our happiness.

"Hawk Roosting" is another poem which can be bracketed with "Thrushes" and "Pike"; it is a starkly objective and brilliantly portrayed image of hawk. What a majestic thought when Ted Hughes tell us that the earth exposes itself to hawk's view for inspection and Hawk proudly feels that he is the lord, he is the monarch of the world and the King can do no wrong. Such is the unchallengeable and indisputable position of hawk:

> My feet are locked upon the rough bark,
> It took the whole of Creation
> To produce my foot, my each feather:
> Now I hold Creation in my foot
> Or fly up, and revolve it all slowly-
> I kill where I please because it is all mine.
> There is no sophistry in my body:
> My manners are tearing off heads—
> ....
> No arguments assert my right.

Hawk is smartly confident and conscious of his being the potentate and need not justify its conduct or position to anyone.

Even the world has remained unchanged and constant since his inception. So shall remain the proud proclamation of this marvelous denizen of Ted's idolized world

I am going to keep things like this.

Who can dare revoke this declaration? Man? Or his entire civilizational dynamic force? It appears that the mood of serious reflection inspires in Ted a painful feeling which gives him a sense of alienation and, in order it find a secure escape, he creates a friendly civilization of peace and purity. There is psychological and biological convincingness in the poet's well-considered conclusion that man is an outsider to God's Creation. There are poets always influenced and moved by the birds and animals and beasts in their own way. We may mention the names of Blake, Wordsworth, Shelley, Keats, Hardy, Yeats, etc. But none has surpassed Ted in his excellence and enviable poetic devices and idiom.

"The Thought Fox", a greatly projected poem initially, is a poem that initiates Ted's poetic process. The title itself is a combination of two nouns making it a compound and the poem is a superb blend not only of the virtues of both in their far reaching characteristics but also it is revelatory of his attitude towards and his aptitude for these idolized creatures, the celebrities in Ted Hughes' poetry. It was declared to be an announcement of the central focus on the themes in the subsequent poetry of Ted Hughes. Keith Sagar has made a brilliant and philosophical analysis of the poem so that when we read it, the richly embroidered images turn into metaphors which become living pictures:

"this midnight moment's forest", "deeper within darkness", show to us the forest on a starless night with "dark hole of a head"

and convince us sure of the relentless persecution of the fox. Ted suggests in his wonder why man has demonized and disgustingly and debasedly viewed harmless creatures like bat, owl, wolf, etc, for centuries. Neil Roberts, too makes such direct reference when he says: "Hughes does everything possible to suggest that the agency of creating the poem has passed from the speaker to the fox." (*Ted Hughes: a Literary Life*, p.21).

The poet may or may not create any landscape for these creatures or, for that purpose, their habitat and they may be in the human habitat, but he does interiorize their life and conduct. The most notable of all is his *Crow* poems. All his poems are richly packed with hurtling action, narrative and dramatic element. This makes him the giant, the most innovative and profoundly gifted greatest poet of the second half of the twentieth century English Poetry till his death. The poems in *The Hawk in the Rain* and *Lupercal* concentrate on the physical vividness of a mimetic sort, in a turbulent world of predatory animals, primitive violence and moments of extreme human endurance—a bloody world governed by impulse and instinct. However, the publication of *Crow* in 1970 provoked a major controversy "as the passages of verse from about the first two-thirds of what was to have been an epic folk-tale". Nevertheless, some reputed scholars and critics thought that it was a major poem, a work of genius which projected "a new hero" as the central symbol, howsoever ironical it might seem. Its instinctively winged dexterity, alacrity, intelligence, speed, sight and the unique ability to fly where and when he wills or wishes are impressively captured with the sharp eye of an artist. It deserves a particular mention here that Ted Hughes admires a genre in oral poetry from the pre-literate world.

Crow: From the Life and Songs of the Crow (1970) is adjudged as "one of his most starling achievements." This is a living portrait of "the adventures of crow from the genesis of life to nuclear apocalypse, presenting Hughes's version of the creation story. The protagonist, the Crow, is at war with the world, including his creator. Throughout his long journey, crow experiences individual and universal tragedies and assesses both human pretensions and life itself with coldly sardonic observation." The poems in *Remains of Elmet* (1979), *Moortown (1979)*, *River (1983)* offer vivid and richly revealing description of animal life and nature and generally project a more positive view of humanity than his previous works. *"Remains of Elmet"* traces the history of Elmet region of England as it develops from an ancient kingdom to modern industrial area. We can fairly conclude that Hughes's poetry encompasses mythology and pre-Christian religion and often presents Christianity as a destructive force. (*Contemporary Literary Criticism*: *Hughes, Ted (Vol.119)-Introduction*)

It is largely felt in the academic and literary circles that *Crow* has entered the poetry-reading consciousness; not only this, its manner or manners have been consciously and widely imitated and parodied.

Anthony Thwaite has deeper and noble insight into the universe-centred heroic position of the *Crow* saying that basically he "has two characters—Crow himself and God. Crow is resilient, resourceful, evasive, built to survive every kind of disaster: he is a protean figure, but these are his irreducible characteristics. God is sometimes his partner, sometimes his adversary or rival, often a passive presence who goes on sleeping while Crow gets up to his gruesome tricks:

> Crow laughed.
> He bit the Worm, God's only son,
> Into two writhing halves.
> He stuffed into man the tailhalf
> With the wounded end hanging out.
> He stuffed the head half headfirst into woman
> And it crept in deeper and up
> To peer out through her eyes
> Calling its tail-half to join up quickly, quickly
> Because O it was painful.
>
> —*Anthony Thwaite*: *Poetry Today 1960-1973* (p.p 45-6)

That is Ted Hughes's version and poetic interpretation of the story of genesis. That is how his civilization beyond the civilization came into being with all its pains and pangs. Such is Ted's revolutionary hit at the very existing patterns of poetry awakening it to the new world of poetry and man. Michael Schmidt pertinently observes, "The century's poetic revolutions begin in polemical experiment and end in polemic plain and simple. Imagism is first a discipline and then a repetitive school; New Formalism an articulate reaction and then a prescriptive orthodoxy." Ted ushered in a new poetic revolution by the innovative use of spontaneously forceful poetic idiom and device in thought-content, spirit and style.

In *Crow's Theology*, Ted says:

> Crow realized there were two Gods-
> One of them much bigger than the other
> Loving his enemies
> And having all the weapons.

And Anthony Twaite questions and substantiates his answer by relying on others. "But what is *Crow* about, beyond its manner? Some have answered 'Survival'—that of the merest subsistence, against mercilessly inimical forces. More nearly, it seems to me, it poses in aggressive terms an old-fashioned theology or demonology—a Manichean duality which Augustine would have recognized...." Hughes smartly raises himself above criticism, even in his assertions because, notwithstanding his repetitive and monotonous rhetorical devices, judged completely as technical constructs with few key words like black, blood, smashed, stabbed, screamed, the reader is convincingly led to believe that not language but message is the medium, so important. There is an impatient rush of thought to rush away from our own to rush amidst these celebrities; this is an irresistible passion!

Finally, we may say that Ted Hughes may not be an ornithologist but he is invariably a bird-watcher, a bird, beast and animal lover, a zoophile. His observation and description, imagizing and idolizing the birds, animals and beasts are a fine, fascinating and enlightening study in anatomizing the language with all words, word-combinations, phrases, idioms, metaphors and even far-fetched comparisons to expose our mind into a new insight into their conduct. It is all rugged, cobbled, rough, piercing, assaulting revealing their resolute will and absolute tenacity to survive with a sense of pride in an inimical world dominated by equally resolute and inimical man. Ted appears to be conveying his message in clear terms and tone to the creation of God—We are created to admire and love with all faults we see here and there.

Works Cited

Albert, Edward, *History of English Literature* (Revised by J.A.Stone) 5th Ed. 21st impression, 1997 OUP, New Delhi.

Bentley, Paul, *The Poetry of Ted Hughes: Language, Illusion & Beyond*, Longman, Harlow,1998.

Contemporary Literary Criticism, Hughes, Ted (Vol.119), Introduction.

Nick, Gammage (ed.), *The Epic Poise: A Celebration of Ted Hughes*, Faber & Faber, London,1999.

Oxford Companion to 20th Century Poetry, (ed.), by Ian Hamilton, OUP, Oxford, New York, 1996.

Pelican Guide to English Literature—The Modern Age, Edited by Boris Ford, Penguin, 1974.

Sagar, Keith (ed.), *The Challenge of Ted Hughes*, St. Martin's Press, New York, 1994.

Sagar, Keith, *The Laughter of Foxes*, Liverpool University Press, Liverpool, 2000.

Schmidt, Michael, (ed), *The Harvill Book of Twentieth-Century Poetry In English*, Published by Rupa & Co, New Delhi, 2000.

Twaite, Anthony, *Poetry Today 1960-1973*, Longman Group Ltd. 1973 publication for the British Council.

5

The Growth of American Dramaturgy in Historical Perspectives

It is a task of tremendous responsibility and a formidable challenge to attempt to trace the origin and the various stages in the evolution of a particular genre in the literature of a particular nation. It not only demands scholarship and industry but also honest and scrupulous approach. Any presumption in handling the major issues involved in the extensiveness of the subject will certainly degenerate into a literary hoax. Also when the limitations of time, space and sources harden the task, some omissions also appear intentionally and unintentionally. It is against the consciousness of these constraints that I have set out on the venture of fleeting view of the historical growth of the American dramaturgy.

The history of the American dramaturgy presents a dismal picture of its development more than a century after America won her political independence on July 4, 1776. However, poetry and prose showed very healthy signs of growth. The seeds of American drama lay scattered here and there on the infertile grounds for a long time. They did sprout into the first cotyledons but did not flourish beyond that. This unhealthy, stifled and haphazard growth can be ascribed to some very obvious reasons. Firstly, America had been relishing and rejoicing in the celebrations of her newly-achieved political freedom. As a result, she was heavily dependent on the British and European cultures. So much so that *Our American Cousin*, a play during the performance of which Abraham Lincoln was stabbed to death in the theatre box in April 1865, was written by a British dramatist, Tom Taylor. Secondly, the prejudice of the puritans against the drama and the theatre continued till the end of the nineteenth century. Even then, a great many plays, mostly insignificant, were produced. These plays did not have the merit of crossing the boundaries of the mediocre. For this impoverished dramaturgy, the neglect of the playwright and the callous indifference of the players and the producers were also held to be accountable. Thirdly, American theatre suffered seriously from romance, melodrama and sentimentality. There was none at that time to blow fresh whiffs of freshness from realism and take up native themes to rejuvenate the art of dramaturgy. Fourthly, some great and popular novels were also used for dramatization. No American play was ever heard to have been staged in England and Europe then.

According to Myron Matlaw, "Before the Civil War, native drama had no artistic stature: the only literarily significant play was a romantic verse tragedy on a much-dramatized theme, George Henry Boker's *Francesca da Rimini*" (1855). Indigenous themes and characters appeared rarely: principally in "Indian" drama, in a few comedies (the best of which was Anna Cora Mowatt's *Fashion*, 1845), and in two popular melodramas, W.H. Smith's *the Drunkard* (1844) and George L. Aiken's *Uncle Tom's Cabin* 1852. It would be germane here to observe that this entire period had been almost barren in the British and European history of dramatic literature also. Ibsen and Strindberg not only revived but also rejuvenated drama. Soon after the Civil War came to an end, Ibsen's dramatic potentiality and genius had already established itself. The American actor's, Joseph Jefferson's, vehicle, *Rip Van Winkle*, continued its tour till his death in 1905. Other such melodramatic romantic star vehicles were American theatre in the late nineteenth century. It included those of Denman Thomson and the dramatic adaptation of Alexander Dumas's *The Count of Monte Cristo* in 1883 by the actors, Charles Fechter and James O'Neill, the father of America's first major and revolutionary playwright, Eugene O'Neill.

By the end of the nineteenth century, great art movements had emerged and were working well in major European countries. Particular mention in this regard may be made of the Theatre-Libre of Paris (1887), the Freie Buhne and Kleines Theatre of Germany, the Moscow Art Theatre founded in 1897, the Abbey Theatre of Dublin and the Independent Theatre of England. They were all successfully experimenting with drama. But there was no such stimulus in America. In the post-Civil War period before O'Neill, three dramatist-managers were the sole driving force of the American theatre. They were the Irish-born Dion Boucicault famous for his long running *The Poor of New York* (1857) and *The Octoroon* (1859), Augustin Daly known for his world-famous company and play *Under the Gaslight* (1867) and David Belasco. It would be a serious omission in the history of American dramaturgy if we do not mention F.H.Murdoch, Bartley Campbell, George Ade, William Gillette and Clyde Fitch, the last of whom was the most popular playwright of the end of the nineteenth century. Though Henry James also tried his dramatic capability, yet Bronson Howard August Thomas and William Vaughn Moody were also distinctive in the field and fairly deserve to be the first great dramatists of America. They presented only scenic realism but were far from the realistic presentation of people and social problems.

It is an undeniable eternal truth that the course of history diverts into fresh pastures and woods when foreign cultural influences are allowed to work liberally on it. The American drama also felt this invigorating and creative experience when some talented young Americans travelled to these European centres in the first two decades of the twentieth century and returned enriched and enlightened to give new directions to the art of the native drama. These young talents preached their newly-learnt dramatic lore at home. The response was also equally enthusiastic. Some community playhouses or workshops came into being all over America in the first two decades of the twentieth century. The Toy Theater in Boston produced plays; Stanford University Theater at Palo Alto in California also engaged itself actively in drama production. A large number of colleges introduced play-writing as courses under the guidance of renowned teachers such as George Pierce Baker of Harvard, Thomas Wood Stevens of Carnegie Institute of Technology, etc. These teachers, theatres and workshops performed radical experiments and revolutionized American dramaturgy. No commercial theatre had ever initiated such changes.

This new movement, however, left its impact on the commercial theatre also. On the other side, the audience relished the freshness of the winds when the newly taught and trained playwrights, producers and players gave their performances. So three major theatre groups emerged in the new theatrical ambience. They were—Washington Square Players established at Greenwich Village in 1915 which later became the Theatre Guild in 1919; the Provincetown Players of Cape Cod also founded in 1915 and it shifted to New York City later. The Group Theater, established by some breakaway members of the Theatre Guild, became active in 1931. These theatre groups earned envious success very rapidly and presented the plays of prominent dramatists like Vincent Millay, Clifford Odets, Eugene O'Neill etc. Maya Koreneva who has done intensive and extensive research in American dramaturgy at the Gorky Institute of World Literature in Russia has very pertinently observed: "American dramaturgy never had the chance to develop gradually with grace. Because of its peculiar development, it could not accumulate artistic treasures; beginning from scratch it immediately set out on an independent path without essentially experiencing a long period of development."

What will be the shape of things to come in American drama is told to us by a great authority on American drama, Joseph Wood Krutch. He says,"The original manifesto of the Washington Square Players was a pastiche of now familiar phrases—" The future of American theatre—experiment and initiative—commercial purposes of managers—not organized for purposes of profit—if you are in sympathy with our aims—Its program was vague and there was no hint of commitment to any social or political program, not even of the enthusiastic concern with the particular variety of moral radicalism associated with the 'free theatre' in England, Germany and France."

One man who had the immensity and profundity of dramatic potentiality and originality, and, without whom, no serious discussion on American theatre can be initiated and who alone enjoys the widest international acclaim as an American dramatist and who alone not only brought about a revolution in American drama but also caused its birth was Eugene O'Neill. And it is by common unanimous consent of the scholarship on the subject that the date of birth of American drama is fixed at July 28, 1916 when the amateur Provincetown Players produced O'Neill's *Bound East For Cardiff.* Thus we learn that American dramaturgy is purely and entirely a twentieth century child. By that time, American literature had achieved a level and a status rightly comparable to the best in European literature. Between the Two World Wars, the finest masterpieces had ripened to maturity in its womb. " The creation of a national dramaturgy was a part of this flowering of American literature and the new artistic perspectives that had opened before it," says Maya Koreneva. Obviously, American dramaturgy was fully prepared to struggle and meet the highly complex tasks ahead. The result was that American plays gained popularity in Europe whereas we hardly ever heard of even one American playthere earlier. This is a commendable achievement in the first and second decade of its existence. In this context, we first mention O'Neill followed by Elmer Rice, Clifford Odets, Irwin Shaw and Lillian Hellman.

This period is conspicuously marked by a variety of artistic trends never before seen and perhaps not to be seen again. Realism tried to depict the truth of the reality of the time. Such realism found its basis in the classical works of Stendahl, Balzac, Flaubert, Tolstoy, Dostoevsky and Chekhov. Other chief artistic tendencies which accompanied it were futurism, expressionism, imagism, dadaism, surrealism and symbolism. It was amidst this "motley artistic panorama" that O'Neill's tensions mounted and realism was doomed. M. Koreneva says, "American theatrical yesterday would give nothing but negative values to O'Neill: things which had to be destroyed and overcome once and for all." Thus O'Neill entered this fierce struggle for a national theatre in which his firm resolve was to "be an artist or nothing." (His own words quoted by O.Cargill et al.)

O'Neill laid the sure foundations of American drama with realism, psychological realism and even autobiographical realism. This true sense of reality alone fulfilled America's dream of a national theater. He dramatized to the audience the crude speech of the sailors, their fights and other cruelties of their behaviour in reality in his sea plays like The Long Voyage Home and The Moon of the Caribbees after the success of Bound East For Cardiff. As O'Neill's vision as a dramatic artist blossomed and ripened, he closely observed the deep-rooted inherent contradictions and conflicts in American reality which completely shun the spiritual values and corrupted man and society and which encouraged inhumanity and injustice and hostilities to art. Such a disgusting reality disturbed the very core of his being. He presented the same with either ironic mockery or profound tragedy in his plays. His strenuous efforts as an artist gave a live presentation of them all on the stage, and his peers and successors—Elmer Rice, Clifford Odets, Paul Greene, Lillian Hellman, Arthur Miller, Tenessee Williams and Edward Albee—were quick to follow the lead and depict the problems in the same vein and fashion. Also it would not be an exaggeration to say that O'Neill gave modern interpretation to Greek tragedy.

Not only realism or expressionism or the classical tragedy or the philosophy of Nietzsche left their influences on him but he set new trends in stylization and performance also. The fact is that he did not confine himself to one or the other basic principle of dramaturgy. *Beyond the Horizon,* steeped in realism, established O'Neill as a dramatist of remarkable skill and vision. He was a successful experimentalist whether he wrote *The Hairy Ape* or *The Emperor Jones* or *Mourning Becomes Electra* or *The Great God Brown* or *Lazarus Laughed* or *Strange Interlude* or *The Iceman Cometh,* to mention only a few. His range of dramatic creativity and potentiality is so wide and immense that the whole American drama to this day follows in his footsteps. John Gassner has paid a rich glowing tribute to O'Neill in these words: "The stature of O'Neill casts a long shadow on the American theater....the height and breadth of the American theater is measured by it. Find fault with O'Neill and you find fault with the entire American stage; find merit in him and you find worth in its striving or straining towards significant drama." With him alone, even today, American drama gains and earns a position of status in the world drama.

The tragic 1930's also made a considerably significant contribution to the growth of American drama. There were really some fine playwrights during this period among whom we may particularly name Maxwell Anderson, S.N. Behrman, Robert Emmet Sherwood, Phillip Barry, Clifford Odets and Lillian Hellman. Anderson successfully and repeatedly wrote idealistic verse drama for the commercial theatres of Broadway. For him, theatre was the temple of democracy and he was uncompromising in his conviction, talent and dedication. A man with impressive accomplishment with all his flaws, Anderson chose to modernize the old conventions instead of breaking fresh grounds. He wrote different kinds of plays which have enduring appeal. He wrote verse histories, *Elizabeth the Queen, Night Over Taos, Mary of Scotland* and also patriotic drama and still there is large variety. All his plays reveal his strong faith in man's individual responsibility, in democracy and his distrust of the government. He enriched American drama with his varied gifts in verse and prose—histories, romances, fantasies, tragedies, comedies and plays of social protest. S.N. Behrman wrote about thirty plays, adaptations and translations. He was a dramatist of great humanitarian concerns and dealt with social problems. Such serious concerns and pre-occupations "hanged his plays from conventional high comedy into a more earnest type of drama." His drama of ideas is not in the Shavian tradition but in the tradition of Congreve and Moliere. Among his well-known plays are *Biography, Wine of Choice, The Talley Method, I Know My Love,* etc. His drama, comedy of manners, is an affirmation of decency and tolerance.

Sherwood, a versatile dramatist, is mostly known for his fifteen dramas, the famous being—*Idiot's Delight (1936), Abe Lincoln in Illinois (1938), Reunion in Vienna (1931), The Petrified Forest (1934), The Ghost Goes West* and *There Shall Be No Night.* All these plays bear the characteristic stamp of Sherwood. Myron Matlaw says, "Sherwood excelled in comedy and history drama, but was equally at home with satire, low comedy, romance, sentiment, melodrama and tragedy." Even Wilder added new artistic life and vitality to the drama of 1930's, though it was confined to the naturalistic protest plays.

In passing, a conspicuous reference is also essential to the left-wing drama or protest drama inspired by the labour union activities. Clifford Odets and Lillian Hellman were important no doubt but Michael Gold and Lithuanian-born Emjo Basshe organized New Playwrights group of which John Howard Lawson, Paul Sifton, E.P.Conkle, Robert Ardrey, etc., deserve to be mentioned. This movement gained historical significance as it added new vigour to the American theatre. Odet's *Waiting for Lefty,* a history-making episodic one-hour drama, was inspired by the New York Taxi drivers' strike in 1934.

The Anglo-American and native dramatists, poets, novelists, critics and short story writers also deserve a place in the history of the American dramaturgy. Just before the War, the emergence of verse drama gave vitality to this genre in America. T.S. Eliot and W.H. Auden and the native playwrights like Anderson who wrote *What Price Glory?* in collaboration with Laurence Stallings earned acclaim and fame. The poets like Vincent Millay, E.E. Cummings, Robinson Jeffers and Archibald Macleish were in the swim. Paul Osborne also wrote plays; *Accent on Youth,* a funny comedy by Samson Raphaelson, is about a dramatist and the theater. Critics like Edmund Wilson, Channing Pollockand Alexander Woollcott; novelists like Dreiser, Gertrude Stein and Scott Fitzgerald; Short story writers like Damon Runyon, William Carlos William, Conrad Aiken also tried their hand at drama, whatever be the level of their success. Among others more successful were Jesse Lynch Williams, Sinclair Lewis, Steinbeck and William Saroyan. *The Night of January 16* by a famous philosopher, Ayn Rand, was a hit mystery drama in 1935. However, Norman Mailer with his *The Deer Park* and Joseph Heller with his *We bombed in New Haven* could not succeed in using their potential as novelists for drama. We cannot afford to ignore Hemingway, Julien Green, R.P. Warren, Faulkner and Saul Bellow for showing a bit as dramatists.

Although leg shows, frothy comedies and serious drama continued to hold the audience to sway, comedy and musicals were the main fare of the theatrical recreations during the World War II and the post-War period. Musicals is considered to be America's most notable contribution to the Western drama. Some of them were lavish musicals and they were superbly artistic blend of drama, music and choreography. Joshua Lagan's *Mister Roberts* (1948) was among the most popular comedies about war. We may also mention other comedies such as Mary Coyle Chase's invisible-rabbit play *Harvey,* Garson Kanin's *Born Yesterday.*

The dramatists who towered above all in the 1940's in the post-War dramatic scene, were Arthur Miller and Tennessee Williams. The scholarship and the audience have sustained interest in these two playwrights even today. Williams does not have O'Neill's diversity of dramatic forms whereas we feel that *Death of a Salesman, All My Sons* and *The Crucible* have been written by different playwrights. This might be said of Albee also for, out of his ten or so plays, only two—*Who's Afraid of Virginia Woolf?* and *A Delicate Balance* have the same structural design. Their drama is an indictment of American society and they depict the tensions and frustrations caused by the evils rampant in social, economic and political systems of America. Life printed on the US Dollar Bill is not what actually the Americans live. Miller's *All My Sons* and Williams's *The Glass Menagerie* dramatize the tensions in the family and both advocate the right of the youth to revolt against their parents. Miller is a patrist playwright whereas Williams is a matrist and the lacerated and the bruised soul is their commonality. Miller's *Death of a Salesman, a controversial modern classic,* and *The Crucible,* family dramas of great social and psychological conflict, had a great influence on the American audience. Tennessee Williams also takes up in all earnestness the social and psychological issues of his time in his famous plays— *The Glass Menagerie, A Street Car Named Desire* and *Cat on a Hot Tin Roof.* He may not be a dramatist of ideas but he is very adept at conveying his sensibilities in an artistic manner. Williams is romantic also in his themes. *The Glass Menagerie,* a memory play, the portrait of a family, depicts a conflict between a romantic idealistic past and the unsavoury present with the sweating struggle for survival. Similarly, *A Street Car Named Desire* is also a soul-shattering experience which portrays the agony, pathos, frustration and destruction of a young woman seeking asylum in her sister's home is raped by her brother-in-law. These plays create a feeling of horror also.

Miller and Williams inspired other dramatists in the 1950's and their influence is seen on William Inge, Robert Anderson and Arthur Laurents. Although O'Neill had become an international star in the world drama, the popular playwrights of the 1950's who couldn't make any worthwhile and enduring contribution to drama are Richard Nash, John Patrick, Gore Vidal. However, it may be recalled that Morton Wishengrad came out with a great play *The Rope Dancers,* a play of sex and psychiatry about a deformed child and her guilty mother in 1959. During this period, there was "the perennial crop of harmless erotic comedies" by Neil Simon, George Axelrod, etc.

Now we observe that American drama took big graceful labyrinthine strides in its advancement to reach the artistic summits of the world drama. In the 1960's, not only Edward Albee's dramatic genius fully bloomed but also the black theatre and the black dramatists emerged as a force to reckon with. Albee turned out to be the most exciting and the most promising playwright. So it seemed. He achieved international acclaim and recognition with his first full length play *Who's Afraid of Virginia Woolf?* in 1962. Earlier he had swayed the avant-garde audiences with one-actors. He was decorated with the 1966 Pulitzer Prize for his *A Delicate Balance.* We may unhesitatingly say that Albee's philosophy is closer to the playwrights associated with the Theatre of the Absurd. Maya Koreneva points out, " His plays often exhibit motives characteristic of this sort of theatre: the tragic estrangement of people, their inability to communicate, the futility of opposing evil as a primary, eternal condition of existence, and the absurdity of human existence." Albee has depicted the events and phenomena concretely in the psychologically complex characters. Martin Esslin, the founding father of the Theatre of the Absurd and who coined this term, did include Albee's plays in this genre with some reservations objecting to the social criticism in the plays of Albee, the feature which is alien to this movement. Even Brian Way writes in his essay *"Albee and the Absurd"*: "The Zoo Story, The Sandbox, and The American Dream, are, on the face of it, absurd plays, and yet, if one compares them with the work of Beckett, Ionesco or Pinter, they all retreat from the full implications of the absurd when a certain point is reached. Albee still believes in the validity of reason...scarcely touched by the sense of living in an absurd universe." Koreneva has observed more pertinently that Albee "has borrowed a good deal from the arsenal of absurd theatre." In this context, it can be safely said that his social criticism is a device suited to the structural basis of his plays. Albee's indispensable belonging to the Theatre of the Absurd has been summed up with a greater insightful understanding by Koreneva in these words: "The grotesque stylization of characters, the omitting of logical progression and links, the deliberate absurdity of dialogue, the use of cliches, the closed structure of the works that emphasizes the static action are all tried devices of absurd theatre, and yet they serve different artistic purposes in the works of Albee."

Other playwrights of this decade who make a name for themselves are Jack Richardson, Sidney Michaels, William Hanley, William Gibson, Frank Gilroy and the distinguished American poet, Robert Lowell.

Last but not least, black drama, black theatre and the Negro playwrights began to emerge as a potent force in the history of American drama in the 1960's and set in it new trends with the other side of realism in American social and individual psyche. There is no doubt that prior to this, dramatists like O'Neill, Connelly and Green did feature blacks sometimes. But now was the time when the black drama, more radical and progressive, was seen in the plays of James Baldwin, Ed Bullins and LeRoi Jones. The militancy of the Black Power Movement towards the end of this decade further influenced it and stylized the writing and performance of drama. So much so that the Black Theatre groups broke away from the white American theatre to perform exclusively for the black audiences. This movement spread its wings outside America also in England, Jamaica, Nigeria, France, etc. and it made a significant contribution to the expression of black identity. In this respect, Lorraine Hansberry's *A Raisin in the Sun* in 1959 was the first major grand success by a black dramatist. According to Myron Matlaw, "It was with the work of LeRoi Jones in the 1960's, however, that black revolutionary drama established its identity. 'Black playwrights' were heard from in growing numbers, and their works started to be widely produced in New York and elsewhere in the United States and abroad."

Among the notable achievements of this movements, we may count Adrienne Kennedy's *Funnyhouse of a Negro* (1964), Ed Bullins' tragicomedy *The Electronic Nigger*, Douglas Turner Ward's satiric short-comedies *Happy Ending* and *Day of Absence*, Lonna Elder III's *Ceremonies in Dark Old Man* (1969). It is more important to name Charles Gordone, cheered as an important new American dramatist, for his *Black-black Comedy, No Place To Be Somebody* in 1969 and it was the first Off-Broadway play to win a Pulitzer Prize. However, what August Wilson has done to this movement, no one else perhaps could do for his message fell like a thunderbolt in American theatre and today, almost three years after his death, its thunderous reverberations have assumed greater dimensions.

In conclusion, we may say that American drama has achieved an assured and envious standing in the history of the world drama in less than a hundred years of its undisputed originality and triumph. Gerald Weales has said that changes in the means of production and in methods of staging, once experimental, have won acceptance.

He adds: "Although these changes have made great holes in the restrictive walls of the realistic theatre, only a few American playwrights have dared to breakthrough, to go out and up. What we need at the moment are playwrights willing to risk a great deal. Perhaps we have a theatre without walls. What we need now is a theatre without bounds." Yes, Gerald wished it in the late1960's and his wish has been fairly fulfilled in less than four decades! American drama, its growth and its tremendous rapid advancement, is characteristic and typically reflective of American temperament in stunning the world with its progress.

Works Cited

Abramson, Doris E., *Negro Playwrights in the American Theatre*: 1925-1959, 1969.

Bullock, Alan (ed.), Oliver Stallybrass and Stephen Trombley, Sec. Edition, *The Fontana Dictionary of Modern Thought*, Third Impression, May 1989.

Downer, Alan S., *Fifty Years of American Drama 1900-1950*.

Gassner, John, *Masters of the Drama* 1954.

Krutch, Joseph Wood, *The American Drama Since 1918*, Revised 1957.

Matlaw, Myron, *Modern World Drama: An Encyclopedia*, Martin Secker & Warburg Ltd., London,1972.

Meserve, Walter J., *An Outline History of American Drama*, 1965.

Mitchell, Loften., *Black Drama: The Story of the American Negro in the Theater*, 1967.

Quinn, Arthur H., *A History of the American Drama from the Civil War to the Present Day*, Revised 1936.

20th Century American Literature: *A Soviet View*, Progress Publishers, Moscow, 1976.

Weales, Gerald, *American Drama Since World War II*, 1962.

Weales, Gerald: *The Jumping-Off Place: American Drama in the 1960's*, 1969.

6

The Elegy and the Elegiac in the Poetry of Joseph Patrick Fernando

Patrick Fernando is considered to be a major force and, of course, the most significant voice in Sri Lankan poetry. It may seem incompatible with his profession as a taxman and a revenue specialist all his life; it is also astonishing. However, a genius works and expresses itself in mysterious ways as it did in J. P. Fernando and as it does in countless others here and there. Son of the sea, groomed well in Western classical lore and literature, keenly and resourcefully interested in teasing social and theological questions, Fernando frequently wrote on them for reputed journals. He had an eye and mind's eyes and spirit wide open and receptive to the luxuriant growth of nature in her full bloom and beauty, and an enthusiastic and vibrant participator in its dramatic performance. Fernando's poetry is a living and enduring response to this all. He had an envious command not only over Sinhalese and English but also over Greek and Latin, and he was beloved to them. His passion for birds and his piercing insight into the working of death is invariably reflected in his poetry, though the Christian themes are also richly handled. "A keen gardener, he loved large trees, foliage plants, anthuriums and orchids. He spent most of his weekends supervising his coconut plantation at Mangala Eliya. His other interests included fish-rearing, bird watching, reading and listening to Western classical music."

Fernando's "meticulous, mannered poetry" was well-inspired and shaped by his western classical learning and literature. These roots have a natural inborn concern for discipline and precision of technique of the classical tradition which he practiced scrupulously. Even in the thick of hostilities of the chauvinist cultural insurgents, Fernando faced and worked victoriously for his roots in the "unhelpful isolation". Perhaps none or nothing can destroy the well-nourished, deep and wide-spread roots though the assaults hurt and bruise.

The dark, gloomy and tragic tone and temper find their overwhelming expression in the poetry of Fernando. It reminds us of J.M.Synge's *Riders to the Sea*, the greatest tragedy written during the twentieth century wherein the playwright has portrayed the high colours of the gloom, the mourning and the tragic. The dominance of the elegiac which counts for its lyrical beauty and excellence of theme and style form the true force and forte of Fernando's poetry. So is its attraction and appeal above and beyond the sensitive. This taxman is taxing his readers with such profundity and immensity; its greater excellence is experienced in its mental and aesthetic satisfaction. His poems are long enough to cover the subject and short enough to reveal it in all its tenderness and grace. We can't venture out into the poetic landscape and horizons of Fernando without being fairly acquainted with the *Bible*, the Greek and the Roman mythology. What adds to his inimitable strength is his stupendous ability to use felicitous phrases, compounds (complex and simple) and condensations. The beauty that emerges out of the elegiac in his poetry is simply stunning.

An elegy is a poem of serious reflection, a meditation, a lament, a mourning over somebody's death. Of course, it has an intensity of a moving, heart-rending and poignant lyric, both at the subjective and the objective level of spontaneous response. In Greek and Roman poetry, it is a poem composed in elegiac couplets. Catallus and Propertius were the major practitioners of this type of poetry. The main feature of elegy is that it expresses formal grief with utmost dignity and decorum in conventional language. Originally, it meant any type of serious personal reflections. Such a lament may be written not only on death but also on any solemn theme or event. In modern literature, elegy is used in wider perspectives in unconventional language but the dignity and decorum are not sacrificed. Roger Fowler says, "Elegy" illustrates a different type of genre-term: ultimately classical in origin, transplanted into modern European terminology only as a word, without the classical formal basis, unrestricted as to structure (except for the minimal requirement that it be a verse composition), overlapping with a number of similarly inexplicit terms (complaint, dirge, lament, monody, threnody), yet conventionally tied to a limited range of subject-matters and styles (death and plaintive musing), and readily comprehensible to educated readers."

During the Renaissance in England, elegy meant to be a poem mourning the death of some particular individual or friend. Edmund Spenser's *Daphnaida* and "*Astrophel—A Pastoral Elegy upon the death of the most noble and valorous Knight, Sir Philip Sydney*" are the earliest examples with us. Even John Donne has used the elegy in the same sense, *A Funeral Elegy* and other such collection of twenty 'Elegies'. Milton bewails the death of King Edward, his learned friend who was drowned in the Irish Seas in 1637, in his *Lycidas*. This is a Monody. Gray's famous *Elegy Written in the Country Churchyard*, Shelley's *Adonais* written on Keats' death, Tennyson's *In Memorium* and Matthew Arnold's *Thyrsis* are the most well-known examples of the elegiac in poetry and they count for among the finest treasures of English poetry.

With all these wide and comprehensive explanations in mind, we study the poetry of Fernando and find that his poems are deftly and gracefully and artistically embrace all these meanings of theme, subject-matter and style. All these lyrics, elegiac and elegies, written in three different phases of his 51 years of richly fruitful life, reserve for Fernando the most coveted position in Sri Lankan English poetry and also an honourable place among the notables in English poetry. Joseph Patrick Fernando has further added to the glow and glory of this genre in poetry with his— *Adam and Eve, The Fisherman Mourned by His Wife, For Paul Claudel, A Symphony in Flowers, The Lament of Paris, Oedipus Solitary, Aeneas and Dido, The Decline of Aspasia, Elegy for December, Meditation over Five Graves, A Fallen Tree, Life and Death of a Hawk, Obsequies of the Late Antonio Pompirelli, Oedipus: The Last Days, One Flock, One Shepherd, A Coat of Many Colours, Pictures for a Chapel of the Passion and Elegy For My Son.*

We may add to the agony caused by gloom, sorrow and mourning to the poet and his poetry by prolonging the list; and it may cure the agony experienced during our journey through those dark and dreadful regions. But let the pain and agony persist to make life more beautiful in its meaning! Fernando's grief is intense and his mourning profound whether he is grieving over the sorrow, agony and death of mythological or Biblical events and characters or the passing away of animate or inanimate objects, human or natural, from everyday life. Fernando's personal grief becomes universal and the universal grief sublimates into a passion for personal grief. Thus in handling the elegiac and the elegy, Fernando ranks among the best in poetry anywhere. Reading Fernando becomes a lasting cathartic experience. Today when life is faced with the severe moral, spiritual and religious crisis of faith in the splendour of life and soul, tragedy seems not only out of context but also meaningless and the absurd in us fails to show its beauty. However, there is no dearth of the sensitive even today. Fernando's artistry awakens even the insensitive.

A Fallen Tree is a very tragic sight; destiny works mutely; nature watches silently and helplessly. How long the giant tree "that overlorded all" suffered silently and seriously from the fatal disease "beyond all lumber lore and reason", only the poor fellows around, for sure, witnessed in silence with an overpowering sense of gloom and grief and surrender—"all the rest stand muted at the giant's fall." But the aftermath was more tragic in its endurance when the wood:

> Shrouds the corpse, for mosses spread and lichens climb
> Over the trunk and round each bruised limb
> Seeking to avert the eye from what they hide.

The poet's lament, a dirge, gains greater poignancy that pierces through our heart and veins when we reach the end. This is a superbly artistic blend of the reality and philosophy, physics and metaphysics. It is an enduring revelation of the animate in the inanimate and the inanimate in the animate. It is an astonishing contrast in its application to human life but the classical touch given to the theme and the sight in this eight-line dirge in the execution of technique and style benumb us for a while till we wake up to the ugly in beautiful, horrible in the pleasant—all on the cozy bed of Mother Earth in the warm and affectionate lap of Nature to the laugh and delight of Destiny. Man away and in isolation from such a delectable experience experiences only the dark misery! A very accurate choice of words and phrases; no superfluity of expression; each word flows with meaning and music and shapes the total picture.

For Paul Claudel, a six-line elegiac, is a lyric of deep personal grief that maintains perfect calm and poise. It has dignity and decorum of its own. Fallen from the inaccessible heights, Paul Claudel merited no comparison to the things that fall or have thorns—roses or kings. So he was a hawk on steady wings:

> Flying on and on and on.

This immortal hawk was born out of the morning air; but it fell "never, anywhere." The fall is neither disgraceful nor depressing. Such a glorification of a human being and vesting it with sublimity and eternity is a mockery of the indifferent and callous destiny. Fernando here transcends his personal sorrow and grief into a momentous delight and deconstructs the human and the superhuman in the face of the divine.

Adam and Eve is a lament, a longing and a painful expression of the grief of the eternal loss of eternal brilliance and beauty. Here we meet the great grand parents of mankind then and the great grand children now—lost in the reminiscences of the beauty and bliss of Paradise. There is no help but endurance and delectable comfort in that. Here is the first landing from the fair and happy home to the mansion in search of which they remain travellers. Adam suddenly wakes to see Eve:

> the brilliance
> Of mountain blooms suddenly come across
> On pale infertile desert ground....

"There was no call upon his mind" "to awake the brutes of blood" provoked by " her rare momentous grace":

> To take her in their hot embrace,
> Ravish her in the foul flesh mud.

Adam was too overwhelmed with ecstasy at the sight to cry her praises in public. Instead he is left to lose himself and live in the sorrow and grief at the loss of "the original trance of beauty first beheld". Gone is the magnificence. They look at each other like the strangely moved and hurt ageing man "pale in the westering light" and feel and wait "in unison death's serpentine advance" with a sense of calm surrender. The poet describes this unfathomable agony of the soul:

> And with infinite gentleness a rich complexity
> Bloomed on their souls, of love and pain and new insight,
> As the last efflorescence is the loveliest on a tree,
> Or as the final movement of a dying fire's dance.

Fernando is a wonderful phrase-maker which shows his superb command over the language used perfectly in the right context. The impact of the discipline of the classical learning is visible in the thematic and stylistic devices used by him.

Oedipus Solitary is a fine meditative poem wherein the philosopher-king of Thebes looks down the memory lane with wide-spread anguish, stricken with grief and guilt. Fernando has depicted the situation in high excellence of compounds and condensations, metaphors and rich images. The life of this hero-king has been the most intensely and passionately dramatic and tragic, a drama of dramas, the story of the greatest sin—physical and metaphysical—ever committed and the severest and the most rigorous self-afflicted punishment. Fernando has picked the situation amidst "the laughter of children mocks the evening's reticence" when Oedipus laments with courageous eyes the sight of his shadowed youth that "lies strangely still, persistent in that posture." Oedipus is now upon the distant ridges of his mind and the mad Bacchanalia haunts him with the:

> Lipstick spread across the prosperous grin of America,
> Or bodies pirouetting at night in halls of Vienna.

All is chilled and frozen into tormenting death and tortuous beyond. Oedipus bemuses

> I do not mourn a loss, I do not weep repentance;
> I only feel my fruitlessness that I who reached the Arctic
> Of all experience of the spirit in the flesh
> Have left no trail, inspired no hope, not even fear,
> Thrust beyond the world of things
> That matter here.

It further enhances Oedipus' agony when he contemplates to lament:

> Youth's exquisite bowl lies shattered on the topmost   shelf,
> Scattered into splinters of pointed pain.

What grandeur Fernando had lavishly bestowed upon this excruciating pain! Oedipus longs to sleep the dreamless sleep of the smashed and splintered age:

> till the youthful hand of God, wearying of time,
> Flings away his toy-world of marble-play,
> Spin, spin you universe, spin out your life.

Similarly, *Oedipus: the Last Days* is a grievous statement of wounds from the very birth through the total gone, not healed by the self-afflicted blindness by piercing his eyes with the brooch of his mother-wife and aching to consciousness the sin and guilt committed under the direction of the predominant blind destiny. His is the tragedy of tragedies, the whole world knows. Fernando has shown rare artistry in capturing and depicting the tragedy in two dozen lines divided into eight stanzas of three lines each with the rhyme scheme—*aba, cdc, efe, ghg*. Who fails to visualize the entire tragedy which lamentably wronged the life of Oedipus, superbly created and crafted human being by the hands of destiny itself. Even in the last days, Oedipus is grappling in a futile manner with the unanswered question eternally haunting man:

> With eyes healed to a thick protective dark, pain gone,
> Burdens of family and state over, and every ambition fled,
> There remains only a concern with right and wrong.

His "Impetuous innocence twisted into public wrong" with two daughters leading him to the city gates to suffer the last but not final banishment:

> "he will pass on." Fernando has enacted the elegiac to reveal
> all before, within and beyond the "protective dark."

Aeneas and Dido is an eloquent expression of a passionate romance languishing in longing and experiencing its waste in grief, a lament and pain. The poem reminds us of Marlowe's play *Queen Dido of Carthage*. Dido, Elissa, was the Queen of Carthage. She passionately loved Aeneas whom Fernando introduces us as:

> Created in the image of God,
> Though sprung from the womb of Eve,

He could impersonate the Lord
And win applause for Dido's grief.

Aeneas deserted her and after his departure, she killed herself.
Later, when Aeneas found her in Hades and recognized her, she
would not speak to him out of feminine grace and vanity. He
observes the grieving and lamenting lovely shade of Dido and
tries to persuade and convince her:

To leave you in that cold grey dawn,
My love, I swear, was not my will;
Yet Heaven pushed me like a pawn
In strange furtherance of its will.

But Dido's face and heart were bathed in grief and sorrow like:

... some rare flower
Caught in a soft infecting wind
Dispetals, fell—she had no power
For speech and fled unanswering.

However, grieving over her hard eternal pride, Aeneas responds
to the decrees of God, sails to a better land and:

He takes a royal daughter's hand,
Enthroned throughout our centuries.

This is how Fernando captures the most tender and painful
moments from the life of these majestic and monarchical figures.

The Decline of Aspasia is one of the most graceful elegies ever
written, a superb example of highly intellectualized poetry, about
one of the greatest wonder-women in the entire history of
mankind. Aspasia stands like a colossus among the women who
moved, influenced, shook, taught, trained and ruled men. This
poem of Fernando gives a very challenging time to the reader,
howsoever scholarly; lifting the layers of meaning explores new
meanings and no number of readings makes it a satisfying
experience. Direct and startling opening captivate our attention
with the immense profundity of language, diction, style, syntax
and thought. Rare use of the marks of punctuation in the sentences
and continuing diction pose formidable difficulties to the reader

to arrive at the intended or implied meaning immediately and even quite after.

> In Western boudoirs the sky applies her lipstick and her
> rouge,
> Waits for the dark-dressed, low-voiced night;
> And in the city sleeping mirrors stir to life and hold
> Images of women pricking hair with pins of gold,
> And men wriggling into collars, creeping into dusted hats.

What a splendid image of the boudoirs! Then follows the scene of dance hall which floods with music and lights-highly pictorial and sensuous to stun us with the plight of Aspasia. She is one:

> Whom time has put on a clearance sale,
> An ageing shop-soiled female:
> Much sought, much loved Aspasia.

That was and this is Aspasia:

> Now she scans the tracks beaten on her empty palm,
> Tracing a descent from Venus' Mount down to where it ends
> In a Babel of prophetic lines
> Whose meaning is now lost,
>
> And in the mirror she estimates the ravages of time,
> Then broods like a wood in twilight
> Deeply hushed,
> The owl iterates his philosophy pacing the roof
> And far away she hears the mumble of a toothless sea.

Years will pass and roll on and on; the moods of the months will work their way into the sill. The beloved skin has shrivelled and cracked like paint on the age-old painting in the galleries of Rome. Such is the dismal and disgusting end to the rich and glamorous and glorious past is unbelievable. But time and destiny, in their own inscrutable way, humble all pomp and pride and power leaving man to trace the meaning of life in that was and this is!

Which scholar of literature doesn't know the story of the love of Helen of Troy and Prince Paris which resulted in the burning of the topless towers of Ilium? Fernando has portrayed the grief of Prince Paris in this sixteen-line elegiac, *The Lament of Paris*:

> When the Greek spear nestles its hot and burning head
>   against my breast,
> And drives the blood to bloom into a red button-hole
>   upon my dress,
> I will ride to Death's night club, I will not come home.

Before his eternal departure, Paris contemplates and laments his grief at the thought of Helen after him. Fernando has revealed the mind of Paris in a poignant present situation and his story in future.

A Symphony in Flowers is a highly tragic lament at the loss of innocence and entrancing beauty amidst the parade of butterflies amidst the chorus of bees when she was sifting the delights of heaven. Later, he saw the same bliss grieving "burdened with the fruition of the flesh" and waiting:

> For the paramour the evening would usher,
> To drain her lovely florescence.

That was many years ago and today, he is strewing the same flowers upon her when she is to descend into the soil to the accompaniment of a sacred tune. It is a poem of the rich splendours of beauty and bloom, dreams and desires, flowering and deflowering-all bathed lavishly in freshness and fragrances that enhance the insatiety in youth, youthfulness and yearning, achieving and reaching consummation till this lovely florescence merged with the sacred melody when she was shut dull to all beauty and bloom so that the ecstatic and embracing earth may burst into a fit of joy. What a living and lovely and lasting contrast of ecstasy and elegy ere losing hushed and haunting reminiscences dipped in the honeyed present. Highly sensual images, compounds and enchanting pictures lead us into a gallery with heard and unheard melodies. A charming magic of the lavish love and lore!

Elegy for December is conspicuous for the conscious use of the condensed and compact phrase and metaphors to build the atmosphere of sorrow, gloom and elegy and contemplate on the agony of love. All is cold and dead around the poet; love alone is alive. He says:

> You alone, my heart, preserve one single fire,
> Deep here, wherein you tenderly enfold
> The girl of my desire.
> Flame fed upon her lips and gentle caresses,
> Light lit by the luster in her eyes,
> She whom you adore above all gods and goddesses
> Beloved unto eternity.

Even the volcanic passion for the girl of his desire is a dirge over December though the rest is elegy. Bitter cold is contrasted with the fiery warmth. The poet has no mind to drown his passion/ fire in the bitter wine in the fashion of the Greeks; it is not the Grecian fire which rises higher and gains sublimity and transcendence as the pining grows stronger and yearning deeper.

Folly and Wisdom is another regret, another grief concealed in folly and wisdom, though the honey-voiced girl and the gentle boy couldn't understand whether they were foolish or wise in keeping the feeling and passion of their love in cold store or burning furnace.

> Exalted eagles drop to earth to chide the sparrow bird.

These lovers have no bitterness or anger and too gentle to realize that they have erred. This short lyric is unique in the treatment of the elegiac.

The Fisherman Mourned By His Wife is a mournful poem on the death of a husband. The wife remembers how their marriage was arranged and how the fisher man trembled to enjoy the bliss of married life. She recollects:

> My eyes were open in the dark unlike in love,
> Trembling, lest in fear, you'll let me go a maid,
> Trembling, on the other hand, for my virginity.

Thereafter, he was always in haste to run to her but it was not to be for long. He was in haste to run away from her. So he did leaving with her his token of love. The poor wife couldn't even console herself-

> Men come and go, some say they understand,
> ....
> You had grown so familiar as my hand,

> That I cannot with simple grief
> Assuage dismemberment.

Meditation over Five Graves is an innovation in the genre of Elegy; it is deep resounding in the mournful notes; no other poet, for sure, has such an artistry in handling the elegy on such a scale— five sections, each for one occupant/s of the grave. This makes a profound variety of grief and mourning in meditation over the death of love and physical passion:

> Here sleep a lovely woman and her lover side by side;
> Each loved and well-fulfilled the physical intent
> ....
> If you wait till the resurrection you might see
> How lovely the tenants of this grave both used to be.

In the second grave, we meet love within the bonds of formal marital love:

> "Here lie a happy man and wife—they enjoyed envy and esteem..." and ruined by enemies of love.

The third grave weeps over and mourns the death of love in virginity:

> Soft buried here beneath three sorrowing marble angels lie
> Three sisters—virgins all—laid out immaculate in lace.

This is "the vacant marriage bed" and the angels over them are their enlightened spirits.

The fourth grave grieves over the wasting influence of misplaced love:

> Unrequited love is here—a man of loyalty and grief,
> Whose solace lay in seeking neither revenge nor relief.
> It is the story of a man who "nailed his heart on a silly girl.
>
> But yet they say great Solomon forgot his wisdom for a slave,
> And lovely Venus lay entranced in the arms of a crippled knave.

The fifth grave is that of a bright man whose head still resounds with his immortal words on love:

So bright in his unfathomed mind to render him profound.

Now his soul well realizes his "primal innocence" and there is understanding full of painful regret:

> ... That love in the abstract sense
> Brings little to a man by way of human tenderness,
> It yearns to walk on earth again and fill the emptiness.

It is a mourning over the unfructified love lost in abstract philosophy which never burst into tenderness and fruition. Such a yearning heart yearns for resurrection to fill emptiness. Unfulfilled love, unrequited love makes life empty and meaningless and even unlived defeating the very divine purpose of creation. The poem is remarkable for condensation of deep thought, immensely packed phrases, profound words resonate to recite and sing the tragedy of love. It is wonderfully reflective and thought-provoking, and it closes on a note of the blossoms of tribute-

> Slowly, the purring processional hearse conveys each day,
> As straw by straw the bird of death building up her nest,
> Another one who loved, to this community of clay,
> Where tired limbs might enjoy their pre-natal rest.

We salute Fernando for such brilliance and his unmatched poetic powers!

Chorus on a Marriage is sad, sorrowful and mournful. It is the story of a sovereign who was a stern disciplinarian and a no non-sense ruler but who secretly sang "the praise of flesh and blood." The poet goes straightforward to tell us:

> Swiftly their love sickened, and patiently,
> Without a murmur, in a year or two,
> Departed. The grave was dug in memory.

The only epitaph was "the world's wild guess"—the wise, the pious and the cynics, all had something to say. When his coronation took place amidst the dizzy dances and celebrations, the attendance of all virtues, the presence of princes and potentates, none had any forecast to make his reign would be so. short-lived.

But Time the Baptist, anointer of kings,
The same as dared destroy Love's gentle breath,
As spared us for recital of these things,
Misled this strong young autocrat to death.
How grieved the kingdom at this second blow!

The footlights on the stage dim to the dimmest for the close of the scene and the song as:

Death hurries in the half-lit dressing room,
Times shuffles in the wings,
God climbs into his old machine,
Half-hidden in the gloom.

Fernando is an inimitable and immortal singer of such choruses; still inspiring love for life and love with the sole stress on the beauty of life. Hence ennobling and elevating!

Funeral Arrangements makes an interesting study in this regard. The poet wants to adore, decorate and embellish her dead body with dew-drenched lilies, mountain red roses, a painted blush on her cheeks so that she leaves us as bride:

....concealing
From us our own stark fear of death.
And let the old with feigned conviction sigh
God takes them young whom God loves best.

All this before a child can begin is curious questioning. Fernando feels tragedy upon tragedy when the priest asks for tithes when burial is a fundamental right. The emotions are charged till the poet leads us to challenge the religious rite.

Life and Death of a Hawk portrays another tragic incident concerning the life and death of a hawk—"monarch of the air" who "ruled the high blue kingdom." The hawk was hawkish in his majestic lofty flights round the sun and his playfulness. The poet is not only wonderstruck but also highly suggestive when he says:

The height he maintained with secret entrance
And exit, kept his colour, size and form
Vague, as befits kings.

But this hawk met a very tragic doom in a mysterious manner:

> Logic snaps; this monarch of the air
> Descending on a kitchenyard for a chicken,
> Was shot, and blundered like a drunkard up a stair.

And for three days, the copse kept hanging in a veil of flies. Destiny works its way like this even with the kings and it remains shrouded in eternal mystery leaving us to our wonderment.

A Coat of Many Colours is a poem of:

> love's difficult harmony-
> Played at last to perfection.

It is a poignant and heart-rending lyric of atrocity in love committed by the narrator's father-in-law,"the old fox" and who "could not offend me further." He laboured hard for seven long years to have her as his wife but was deceived by "the old fox." who commanded another seven years' of labour and the narrator's love became more passionate than ever. Their love story can be read in the book of their lives. However, the next page of the book assigns him two wives, and two more women. Thus the story went till the narrator and the writer of this book met beyond the grave. When he questioned the biographer about himself, he vanished into the dark air saying "that the task of true and keen observer/ Constumed all his life." Amidst all this, he "wove the coat of many colours." It is an elegy on the death of love and life.

Elegy for My Son resounds with a deeper note of pain and agony causing lifelessness at the colossal loss of the poet's admiration, beauty, pride and love by "some strange excess of love" of earth, wind and sunshine and they work as usual and:

> Calm as the conspirators after the deed
> Driving me to almost believe nothing
> Has happened. I am the tree that's gone,
> That tree and I being one.

In fact, it is not his son, "the young tree" but "I am the tree that's gone." The poet feels that:

> There must be some terrible power
> In the earth and wind and sunshine

How else could the young tree,
A favourite of these three
Sicken in a single day and die?

Fernando felt totally broken when his youngest son died in 1980 and he could not endure the strain and shock for long and he died in Jan. 1982. He would stand in the empty places brandishing his thoughts wildly and bursting into sigh and song at the memory of this wild incident "as if nothing has occurred." How haunting, tormenting and tragic that we have to create the illusion of disbelief to solace ourselves in a highly sensitizing situation! Why should Destiny put us through such killing trials? There is no answer; we are left to reconcile even by welcoming death which comes slowly and painfully in such a situation. This elegy is a subtle literary and subtle masterpiece.

Finally, we may conclude that grief, gloom and grimness, mourning and reflection are all-pervasive in the poetic landscape of Fernandes; he avoids cautiously and artistically the blame-game for this sorry mess most of the time, though it becomes irresistible also. The study poses serious difficulties to the serious reader on account of the fair and abundant acquaintance of the poet with the Western classical languages and literature which has influenced richly his literary devices and which is conspicuous more than the thought-content and also determines the expression of the same. The sorry and the tragic mess is neither disgusting nor depressing; with the basic dignity and decorum in his poems, they become an ennobling and elevating experience in tone and temper. Their bewitching grace inspires lasting reverence for life and its Creator and its Mover. His observing eye moves among the birds, objects of nature and human beings and he depicts their physiology and psychology as they build and determine their relations with life in the totality of its working under the convolvuous supervision of the Dark and the Divine; his artistry is subtle, envious and inimitable. This is the world which inhabits the queens, kings, clerics and soldiers, ordinary mortals and objects, animate and abstract, and are seen grieving and mourning and meditating over the losses—ethereal or temporal!

Works Cited

Fernando, Patrick, *Selected Poems, Three Crowns*, OUP, New Delhi, Ed. 1984 (Text Used with brief Introduction—A Note on the Poet and the back cover note.)

Hamilton, Ian (ed.), *Oxford Companion to 20th Century Poetry*, Oxford Paperback Reference, OUP, Oxford New York Ed. 1996.

Fowler, Roger (ed.), *A Dictionary of Modern Critical Terms*, Routledge India Edition, Reprinted 2005.

Kennedy, X.J., Dana Gioia, Mark Bauerlein (eds.) *Handbook of Literary Terms—Literature, Language, Theory*, Pearson Education, India, First Impression 2007.

7

Multidimensional Props in the Poetry of Mahendra Bhatnagar

Mahendra Bhatnagar is seemingly an easy poet. But he is not. The caravan of images keeps constructing thoughts of varied hues. Passion adored with simplicity, spontaneity, stillness and sonority—sole delight of poetry anywhere—baffle the reader of Mahendra Bhatnagar. These characteristics reveal less the style, more the spirit and subject of the poetic creations of Bhatnagar. The subtle artistry of even the translators of his poems, with all their wealth of linguistic, language and situational equivalence and the excellence of their insight has faltered at most of the places, though their sincerity deserves all appreciation. That is why the translations of the original are a rare delight and its near-accomplishment is still rarer. The difficulties in such a venture emerge because of the complex intermingling of the philosophy of the metaphysics and the physics of daily life handled with excellence, conscious and unconscious, by Mahendra Bhatnagar. Maybe the scholarly translators also experienced the bumpy rides on the roads, which appear smooth and uncobbled, to Bhatnagar's citadel on the wings of their own poesy. Once the journey begins on a happy note with a flowering heart, soon the road is seen branching off into different directions. And we move on the horns of dilemma. Even then, we reach there huffing only to relax after a good sleep amidst fresh and fragranced breezes blowing across the poet's landscape.

The profundity and the intensity, the richness and variety of passion and pain, yearning, fulfilment and frustration of love, melancholy and despair of life—all incessantly lead to dreams and destinations where man is eternally seeking eternal solace in his emotional entanglements, rational unfoldings and revelations, spiritual enlightenment, hope and faith. These are the inexhaustible treasures in the poetry of Mahendra Bhatnagar. What astonishes more the curious and the serious reader of his poetry is how Bhatnagar resolves these contradictions pertaining to the existential issues of the everyday life of the high and the mighty, the humble and the meek. His asphyxiated soul releases itself with the dare and the strength of its convictions and regales the audience with its liberated, luscious, lascivious, lurking and longing fancies.

If romance means the love of the far-off, if romance means love of the open fields, challenging high mountains, rocks, infinite star-studded skies, if romance means sweat of the soil fructifying into dreams, if romance means the betrayal of the beloved's love to embrace the full bloom of the cosmic love, light and colour, if romance means the youth and the youthful venturing out to seek fresh pastures, if romance means to dream and enjoy the maddening fragrance of the beloved's beauty, if romance means to empathize and work for a life of freedom, dignity and happiness for the suppressed and the storm-tossed, if romance means to have a rendezvous with death and let him caress you and be caressed in all preparedness, Mahendra Bhatnagar may have few peers but no superior seems to be in sight. Bhatnagar weaves a splendid pattern of enchanting colours and images reminding us of the romance of the Renaissance and the Romantics of English poetry like Spenser, Shelley, Keats and even beyond that—Tennyson, Morris, Rossetti and Yeats. Dr. Vidya Niwas Mishra in his Preface to the Selected Poems of Dr. Mahendra Bhatnagar-1 remarks: "Mahendra Bhatnagar is Browning, Shelley and Maykovsky welded into one, he is a visionary, he is a comrade-in-arms and he is an architect."

Mahendra Bhatnagar's relentless pursuit of beauty and wisdom to explore the meaning of truth and reality as commonly believed and the philosophical truth is the marked characteristic of his poetry, though it is tinged with lament and elegy at times. Patricia Prime in her understanding of Bhatnagar's poetry, Selected Poems of Dr. Mahendra Bhatnagar-2, has aptly observed, "His poetry is a combination of sublimity and wisdom, and is a way of exploring the meaning of subjectivity and of pursuing philosophical beauty. The poet figure is presented as a humanist, visionary and compassionate ideologist. Spiritually-minded, and open to the greatness of feeling and experience through such vistas presented by the Indian landscape and its people, Bhatnagar's work offers a relentless and vitalized search for the fullness of human experience, and the fulfilment of destiny...."

His *Selected Poems-1* (40 Poems) and *Selected Poems-2* (25 Poems), *Death Perception, Poems for a Better World* are indeed a rich harvest from the ageless fields of poetry. His poetry can be categorized very conspicuously as under:

a) The poetry of nationalism, patriotism, the poetry of rejuvenation, regeneration and resurgence; the poetry of hope and faith and message of the New Age, the Golden Age for the masses living under repression and suppression a life of total denial; this may also include the poems for a better world;

b) The poetry of youth and youthfulness with the undying and living spirit and enthusiasm for adventure for an enduring life;

c) The poetry of personal sorrow, love, beauty and romance;

d) The poetry of Nature in her varying moods and fancies at different times of the day and in different seasons; and

e) The poetry of death.

A poet's chief concern is the dilemma of man under various pressing and depressing situations. An ordinary man with his ordinariness of situation may find the triumphant emergence quite difficult or even the escape-route a blind alley. But the poet, gifted with the insight and farsight, overcomes the crisis caused by the conflicting interests, finds progressive movement pleasant in faith and the message thus transcends. Social, economic, political and religious awakening in man has always created a transitional phase in the general set up of life. Such a transition leaves its deep marks and scars on the value system also which sets in a new era. People prosper and seek happiness in their shared experiences of matter and spirit but these glitteraties, with all their material and intellectual attainments, suffer miserably from their moral and spiritual impotence. This not only disturbs but also aggravates the crisis in everyday life and living. The poet alone is alive to his concerns and the poetry is born. This is how the poetry of Mahendra Bhatnagar is born. Dr. Suresh Chandra Dwivedi, in his "Preface to *Selected Poems of Dr. Mahendra*

Bhatnagar" says very aptly, "He is endowed with the gift of free imagination dedicated to bring about change in our soulless, heartless, dead, disintegrated, disunited, disillusioned capitalistic world where common man is foredoomed to be exploited, cheated and looted at every step." As a champion of the common mass of downtrodden mankind, the poor peasants and workers, Mahendra Bhatnagar not only indicts but also condemns and crushes the forces in the establishment or outside it. Dr. S.C. Dwivedi observes, "He is alert, careful, and cautious, sometimes reminding us occasionally of Brecht, Auden, Pablo Neruda and of Carl Sandburg.... Like them, he is the spokesman of the people, and he employs a rare sensitivity, a rare intellectuality and a rare humanity."

The poems of resurgence have message of hope, faith, understanding, goodwill and humanity. These poems transform us and regenerate and rekindle our faith in the basic goodness and dignity of man as man. These poems awaken us to even the need for a rebellion against what degrades and debases and also dehumanizes us and sounds a clarion call to the ignorant and the suppressed to wake up from their aged slumber, open their eyes to the new dawn of freedom and life. Mahendra Bhatnagar is at times painfully aware of the dismal and bleak situation around and his conscience as poet shakes him thoroughly to attend to the call of his duty. "Lust for life", "Reap the Paddy", "Woman Reborn", "Lose Not Your Heart", "Vision", "Not Alone", "Life-Stream", "Future", "Light", "Conviction", "The Firmament Will Change Its Colour", "With Flags of Peace", "Gala of National Celebration", "The Masses", "Resurgence", "For the First Time", etc., are a few such poems as are packed with Mahendra Bhatnagar's rock-like faith and convictions in the glory of the nationalism, patriotism, humanism whose resurgence will give birth to the sanctified beings who alone will inhabit the New Age, the Golden Age of the dreams of the prophets and visionaries. This Age will be free from injustice, exploitation, loot, inhumanity, atrocity and parasites. The manifesto of the poet's faith divine that love alone is the guiding and leading force of human life since and till eternity, though "The death's orchestra plays on." This is expressed in "Lust For Life" wherein the chief burden of the song is:

The man lives on
By the cravings of love.

The seeds of world's resurgence now find fulfilment and fruition and their "fragrance embraces the whole universe." The tragic plight of even "Woman Reborn" is purported to be a poem of regeneration and emancipation of woman, notwithstanding the fact that it remains a far-cry in the din and pandemonium of Women's Lib. However, "Lose Not Your Heart", a song of rebellion sings on a note of high optimism:

> Your destination itself will arrive one day
> And meet you half way!

That is why the poet's "Vision" is a pledge for the realization of those dreams and ideals. On this pilgrimage, Mahendra Bhatnagar is "Not Alone". He is so self-assured that he asserts

> I am not alone,
> Not alone am I,
> The resurgent age is with me.

This is a poem of message for the New Age in which his optimism sparkles with a rare glow; this is a poem of faith and confidence which creates the atmosphere of constant cheerful movement of myriads of men with inexhaustible energy advancing towards the golden blooming world on the splendid peaks of liberty unhaunted by even by the remote shadows of despair and helplessness. It is today and today alone—undying today becoming forever! This is to be the ultimate fulfilment of God's plan where

> Green, red, yellow and rosy gardens
> Are in full bloom today!
> Man is being initiated into humanity....

"Life-Stream" sings:

> The new song of life's revolt!
> A new song of creation
> ....
> On the wall of the age
> Descends a brilliant crimson light,
> Of conviction bold and glamour rare!

Imagistic pattern here is more spell-binding than the thought-content.

The poet feels in "The Future" that man's future path is enveloped in limitless darkness and thick darkness governs it. We can easily see through the mind of Bhatnagar working in symbols and understands that there is needed bright light, the floodlight. He wants to hear the laughter of every man in his roaring spirits. So:

> And let hopes bloom
> Of a future happy and glorious!

His unflagging faith and optimism are further strengthened when his firm, bold convictions anchor his spirit. In "Conviction", Mahendra Bhatnagar says:

> The tiny lamp of man's undying faith
> Has flickered strong as ever!

His conviction sees the transitional darkness vanishing:

> And wrest from heavens
> A rosy dawn of life new!

There is sure to be a new awakening, new resurgence, New Age, the Golden Age when "The Firmament Will Change its Colour" and "The Flags of Peace" will reinstate our strong faith in "peace and humanity". The innocent dreams of "Resurgent Man" will re-write the history of the world with its aglow with love, freedom and dignity, understanding and brotherhood. All walls dividing man against man, man against God, shall collapse or stand demolished. This planet will become the habitat of sanctified beings working for the evolution of cosmic civilization. The poet can see a new awakening blazing and the world's history taking a turn. So:

> From the world will banish
> The dense darkness of sufferings,
> And the close atmosphere of dejection heavy!
> Surely will the firmament take a new colour!
> —"The Firmament Will Change its Colour"

The jubilations of national liberation, "the eventful day", bring forth "the soldiers of freedom universal" and "This is the day Universal resurgence/ This glorious day/Of the famished, the naked and the suppressed!" The ecstasy of the poet is overwhelming:

> Impediments have turned friendly,
> Magnificent is the current of history!
> That is the landmark of Victory!
> —"Gala of National Liberation"

History bears ample testimony to the enduring truth that masses are never lost in age-long slumber otherwise the era of dark despair and despotism would not have died so soon and "the myriad lamps of life sublime" would not have been lighted to "to sow the seeds of vibrant life on earth." It is always the awakening of the masses, the thunder of the "collective voice" that fructifies the vision of the prophets of mankind. Mahendra Bhatnagar has given fine, splendid and subtle ex-pression to the working of the divinity of life in the universe age after age in his poem after poem. Of course, Bhatnagar's leftist leanings also come to the fore when he asserts that "the demon of capitalism" is the root cause of hunger, starvation, suffering and misery. Then we feel constrained to ask ourselves, and also the poet, if the God of Communism has ever succeeded in alleviating and mitigating these social and economic ills and ailments! There may not be an answer to this question, and if there is any, it will be the subject of futile heated controversy, but the poet sees the wonderful resurgence

> A new flame is blazing in every direction;
> Life is lit up with red twilight.
> ....
> The age and the civilization have taken a turn
> The creeper of culture is blooming with flowers new.
> — "Resurgence"

Again, in another poem,"For the First Time", Bhatnagar blows the bugle of the New Age fight for human rights; a call of the red revolt for the liberation of the common man trodden down since ages. He says:

The new age is busy struggling
For the rights of all,
The coming years will follow suit,
The world will stand guard
On rights of all people!

So there is no reign of terror, no king, no beggar! He is right that concrete convictions never collapse. His poetic rebuke to Mao and Chou are also his message of national resurgence. Similarly, "O Winged Steeds of Destiny" is a poem of challenge and indomitable will as sons of the soil and the toil show their determination coupled with confidence to lead destiny and shape up their own. They have the will to achieve the unachievable with the virtues of steadfastness, perseverance and endurance to take away even the brilliance of stars to adore our daily life. The poet says:

O winged steeds of Destiny!
We will hold thy bridle
And give ye direction!

"Gift of a Lively Faith" is a loving welcome to the dejected and the discarded as he is gifted with a lively faith. In "The Offshoot":

The brilliant sprouts into a new life!

This is also a poem of resurgent life in a revolt against whirlwinds. In "We Know it Well" we find:

That lightning flashes not in the blaze of noon!

"Stop It" — the very title is a command; this is a poem of forceful but silent protest against starvation, misery, suppression and atrocity. Mahendra Bhatnagar uses dreadful images of exploitation, social and sexual, because, in such a disgusting and dehumanizing situation, all slogans and appeals of peace and faith and love sound hollow and dirty and carry no meaning. He says:

The naked carcass of culture;
When your vulture teeth are red
With blood of the teeming millions
And your breath smells of deflowered virginity...

Hence the poet makes a wonderful appeal to the helpless, hapless and exploited millions to open their eyes and see the glimpses of the new purple dawn with a new message of bright cheerfulness and happiness for themselves. This is a message of the New Age full of optimism in the better times. The title, "Poems For A Better World", is quite illusive from this dimension as the poems here are mostly personal though the poet is fully conscious of his chief concern and tension—a better world for all human beings. His poems like-"The Bigots", "Invoking Modern Man", "In 1986 A.D.", "The Other Age", "Dictum", "Someone Unknown", "Corruption", "Trickery of Votes", etc., all deal with the issues that pertain to our daily living and are really essential to the life of rejuvenation and resurgence.

Thus we see that the images of resurgence, regeneration and rejuvenation are the potent virtue in the poetry of Mahendra Bhatnagar and they lend charming vigour to his compositions. They are the message of conviction born out of courage to face and live life. The determined and rebellious mind frustrates the designs of the forces of destruction. However, it cannot be attained unless the strong unfaltering feeling of youth and youthfulness is there. So the poet adores such a state of body and mind in some of his poems, the songs of eternal youth. His "Youth", is an undying assurance in this regard. Here, he is a singer of eternal youth, its enthusiasm, its bubbling energy, its ever-rising aspirations, its ever-fresh adventures and the spirit to reach the unreachable passing on the legacy of newly-emerging beauties to their inheritors, liberally and lavishly. He says:

> From time immemorial the orchestra of youth
> Has been playing on
> And shall ever play
> The new melody of resurgent life!
> ....
> But the light of youth
> Shall never grow dim!
> Time shall pass away
> But youth will endure!

He also advises youth not to languish itself away in romantic fancies and must not be simple and sentimental but work for the realization of dreams of a fresh, golden smiling life!

How can a poet ignore or be deaf to the voice of his conscience and also his heart yearning and smouldering under strains of unfulfilled desires, hopes dashed, dreams gone sour and romance reduced to lackluster sparks in ashes? No poet can be completely impersonal and it cannot be possible for him or her to be objective. May be his impersonality or objectivity are emerge out of his personality and subjectivity. T.S. Eliot rightly observed that "Poetry is not a turning loose of emotion, but an escape from emotion; it is not the expression of personality but an escape from personality. But, of course, only those who have personality and emotions know what it means to want to escape from these things." ("Tradition and the Individual Talent"). Mahendra Bhatnagar is also deeply entrenched in his personal sorrow, love, beauty and romance in his poems and finds outlet and feels comfort in nature in her different moods and fancies at different periods of the day and seasons. When the poet's mind is torn and tormented by some "Dilemma", he feels overwhelmed to express himself in the light of the soul. He questions himself:

What's this weariness?
That leaves inert every limb, every nerve!

Deadened is the mind to sensations all,
Heavy and tired are the eyes with sleep!

His soul is fatigued and its melody finds no echo even in heaven. Even his firm convictions melt and life's paths are beset with difficulties and thorns. It is a grim reality and it is no longer an illusion. Should he surrender or use all the might of the soul to fight stark reality? The poem is loaded with Keatsian echoes, note of sorrow and melancholy marked by irresolution. All is wrought out here of the images flirting out of his lavish mind and the reader is fleeced into the overflowing beehive guarded by the mother bees posing danger and providing delight of "sweetness and light."

In "Light the Lamps", the bitter and sweet of life; the sour strains cloud the silvery bright sun-shine and the star-spangled skies of the poet's life; and he, like Meera, "Drained the cup of poison to the dregs", yet it failed to dampen the ever-thirsty spirit.

Dear! The love is still alive with all its aspirations,
Steeped in the flowery sweetness of spring,
Several nights of enchanting mad moon still remain,
....
Smile and smile a little
And be with me, my company!

Mahendra is romancing freely with moon and moonlight in "To the Moon" and "Moonlight". The very opening of the former leads us into a life of sensations:

Please smile not and tempt me thus,
Or else I shall kiss your cheeks!

He is enchanted by the lavish beauty of the moon "Where dance the naked damsels". Then he says in "Moonlight":

This moon-light speaks not to me none knows why,
Fills the heart with strange nectar of love, this
Moonlight!.

These are highly picturesque poems reminiscent of the pastoral moonlit nights in the poetry of Coleridge and where life has not been assaulted and bruised by the jungles of concrete enveloped thickly by the dust, dusk and soot or threatened by terrorists, political or religious. Mahendra Bhatnagar is frequently a poet of fresh moods and memories in "No Grievance" and in "Conviction", we see the blush and shyness of the full-blooded love of youth and it is all a graceful sight with not even a remote reflection or shadow of physicality. "Day-Dreaming" is a lyric of intense of intense love and beauty, a superb example of tension, intention and extension. He says:

Like a love-lorn bee,
I've only kissed and kissed.
The buds, bright, ravishing, drunk—
And drenched in honey!
How tormented am I
By your beauty!

"Betrayal", another poem of beauty, romance, love and lust, is a betrayal of the beloved's love to hug the cosmic love to find "a new kingdom of joy and smile." "Accept Me" is a poem of love in all its purity and brilliance. He says:

My wishes:
Like the twinkling stars
On the breast of the blue!

Then—My passions; My feelings:

Like the most beautiful garlands
Of red roses
Fresh, fragrant and blossoming!

He offers these all in adoration to her persona of love and idolization, celestial beauty! We roll in romance in other poems— "The Worship of Art", "A State of Mind", "Life", "Through the Unwanted Moments", "The Irony of Fate", "How to Suffer Pain", "The Incredible", "Who Are You?", "A Submission", etc. They all give to us a relish of romance and beauty—lusty and gusty! Almost all the poems here are the poems of desires and dreams and hopes and happiness. Mahendra Bhatnagar has the cardinal feeling of the song, music and beauty of life but this crashes against the inevitable pains, agonies, sighs and tears. The ironies of fate awaken Bhatnagar to the dread:

Oh, Providence!
That the body is tightly tied with countless snakes
And is encircled with sharp thorns;

"The Incredible" is a poem of the life of loneliness without love and romance. Such a life adds to the woes, pains and misery verging on the tragic; the poet, the actor, the hero, the performer, the singer—all alone on the stage of the auditorium completely empty of the audience and the spectators. Singing in broken voice his own requiem from where come out the notes—"so pathetic, monotonous and uncharming." However, from the background appear the intoxicating images of the divine dancers and belles, and they, vanishing so sudden and so fast further aggravating the tension of loneliness and horrifying the romance of emptiness.

In fine, we observe that Mahendra Bhatnagar leads us from the sowing season in the fields of life instilling and enthusing mankind with new hopes, aspirations and dreams to the beauty and lore of ripening and the ecstasy of rich harvests—all a fruit of ever-adventurous human youth, leaving behind the stubble plains whereon we walk barefooted collecting the leftovers passing on into the dusk and dread of wintry night. With this, we move from pastoralism, retreat into medievalism and then to antiquity and eternity!

8

Samskara—Happiness of the Absurd

Although *The Myth of Sisyphus* poses mortal problems, it
sums itself up for me as a lucid invitation to live and to create,
in the very midst of the desert.

— Albert Camus in Preface to *The Myth of Sisyphus*.

U.R.Anantha Murthy says that *Samskara* is "A Rite for a Dead
Man." Of course, by "rite", he means *samskara*. *But the question,
is who is dead—Praneshacharya or Naranappa?* It appears that the
novel portrays life-in-death and death-in-life with subtle
overtones. This short novel depicts nothing but death in the
physical as well as metaphysical sense, and that, too, on an epic
scale. On the surface, it is Naranappa who is dead and the chief
concern of the novelist is to lead to a pragmatically acceptable
solution through the philosophical and scriptural rigmarole to
make an honourable provision for a rite for a dead man. And it
is his artistic failure that even after the intellectual, moral, spiritual
and physical odyssey of "the crest jewel of the Vedanta", the
dominant issue remains unresolved. The protagonist and the
antagonist remain a formidable challenge to each other. And the
antagonist, perhaps a symbol of the turbulent force of the
changing value-system of the decadent and putrefying society
whose daily conduct and life are determined and enforced by the
dark irrationality without least regard or scant respect for the
individuality and the individual aspirations and his obdurate
refusal to stay within the fold, runs away with a triumph that
mocks them all.

All, including the spiritual leader, head and guide of the
community with all his nobility born out of his self-imposed
suffering and misery to maintain and assert the validity of his

proclaimed and estimable image, are ever ready to excoriate and, if possible, pillory Naranappa and bring him within the framework of their own fancy. Since they are all severely afflicted with the incurable psychic impotence and they themselves are consciously and secretly a prey to what they indict as vices and sins in Naranappa and dread his daring exposure, can't help sheepish and cowardly behaviour. It is astonishing and even shocking to think and imagine if the guide-light of the *agrahara*, Praneshacharya, is living as a human being or if the basic human instincts are alive in him. Mechanical performance of family rites and religious ceremonies in his daily life without any conspicuous fruitful meaning do not serve any social or moral purpose. Intellectually dead, spiritually paralyzed and morally decayed community of these brahmins of the *agrahara* expose themselves in their true colours when the issue of disposing of the dead body of Naranappa comes up for open discussion. Anantha Murthy has shown remarkable honesty in launching a well-planned sensitive attack with a set strategy. Though he had to face the wrath of raised eyebrows, flaming tongues and rusted nibs,they failed to dim the light on the spot. Rather it kindled other corners enveloped in ages of darkness.

The immediate issue of cremating the body is lost in the din of discussion on the non-issues pertaining to the brahminical code of conduct of the dead, his relationship with the faithful members of the clan, his brahminical status after his death. Meaner and debased passions are expressed without restraint. We are told about their hypocrisy, greed, jealousy, libidinous desires with the naked eye of the artist. Naranappa's low-caste wife, Chandri, rouses the sensual and sexual desire of Durgabhatta whose "connoisseur eyes" feel tempted to swallow this precious object inside-out. He remembers Vatsyayana's *Kamasutra*, Matsyagandhi and the brahmin poet, Jagannatha, who married the Muslim girl and composed verses about the alien's breasts and felt like quoting them to the barren brahmins. Lakshmana whose wife's sister was married to the deceased also closed his eyes when his anti-brahminical conduct was audaciously exposed. But his wife, Anasuya, was voraciously eyeing the gold jewellery—four-stringed gold chain, thick gold bracelet—worn by Chandri; she hurled mouthfuls of curses and abuses on "this evil witch". Anasuya wept loudly, boiled over and cried. Garudacharya was also angry and mischievous. He involved Praneshacharya in a scholarly and spiritual conflict. Everybody in the *agrahara* disowned Naranappa. So none wanted to bear the brunt and burden of performing the last rites on his dead body. After all, Naranappa did everything strictly forbidden by the brahminical code, and that too openly to ridicule the impotence of all other members of the community! He also challenged the acharya on the total futility and superfluity of brahminism as practised and preached leaving the "crest jewel of Vedanta" witless. We can realize the agony in his words when he says, "Let's see who wins in the end—you or me. I'll destroy brahminism, I certainly will. My only sorrow is that there's no brahminism left to destroy in this place—except you." Even the child widow, Lakshmidevamma, has been tortured to misery by this very brahminism and she speaks of Naranappa as a "golden man" and comes down heavily on these brahmins seeing the dead body rotting in their midst, "Rama, Rama, the times are rotten, rotten. Brahminism is in ruins. Why don't you shave your heads and become Muslims, why do you need to be brahmins, you!"

Yes, it is the challenge of the dead to the force that was once a source of happiness here and sublimation there! It is now a corpse of philosophy, being used as a beacon light to guide and shape the headless here and hereafter. The call of the dead is a trumpet. The novelist also appears to be consciously emphasizing that the will and aspirations of the individual are not only more potent but more relevant and valid than the obsolete value system. Those who are responsible for running such a system must take care that it is nourished with the simmering discontent before it begins to burst at the seams and explodes.

All our knowledge and learning are meant to bring about a pleasant qualitative change in our own life and in the life of the community to which we belong and, more so, the community which we lead and whose spiritual enlightenment is our accepted responsibility. Praneshacharya is out of complete harmony with himself and with the community. He wins nowhere though we find him in a win-win position in the beginning. He is undoubtedly equipped with the armour of the total knowledge of the law books and the scriptures but remains without their light till the end. That is why this well-grounded and well-versed *Acharya* fails and falls in actual battle, inner or outer. In changing the course of the life of Naranappa according to the holy doctrines, in finding or offering a solution to the very immediate issue of providing the last rites for his own challenger or even of his learning and supreme estimation, we find it hard to digest *Acharya's* miserable failure in times of stress and strain.

Not only this, the post-Chandri *Acharya* is more pusillanimous than ever. We simply wonder if he has the will or courage or conviction to participate in life at any level. The Riddleman Putta and the Prattling Putta, the living participator in the show/s of life, remains with Praneshacharya throughout the third section of the novel. He feels irritated, haunted and pestered by him everywhere and tries to dodge him to get rid of him. But he is Putta and must do his best to involve his wayside companion actively in the joy of the romance and the drama of everyday human life. His serious concern for this uncreative learned man without any conspicuous selfish reason has not been made clear by the novelist anywhere. However, we can understand his psychological compulsion. Putta cannot see through the mind of this learned brahmin though we see clearly through the revelation of his interior self how fear-stung he is to face the world seen and enjoyed by Putta. The *Acharya* is looking for escape-routes to a life free from the contradictions, conflicts and the crisis of conscience. He entangles himself in the webs created by his own fancy and self-killing thoughts and actions till, we are told, his return to Durvaspura to make an honest confession to his orthodox community. He tried to seek the prop of Chandri also in this regard but could not. *The Acharya does not have even the foresight to realize the consequences of such a confession—how he would be ridiculed and jeered at and further that the level of his sensitivity would lead him into a fatal disaster.* Notwithstanding the refreshing, revitalizing, rejuvenating and restructuring images and experiences interspersed throughout the novel, with the frantic bid to remove the pall of gloom and grimness, Anantha Murthy deserves all praise for retaining the dignity of his artistry and closing the novel on a meaningful, fruitful and creative suspense for the magnificence and magnanimity of the reader without expecting anything from him and leading him to believe the possible solution.

Anantha Murthy has woven so much in the design of the novel that the thematic concerns are closely interrelated with the structural analysis. The ending of the novel remains a puzzle, an enigma and a thirst for the already slaked throats. In this fascinating and philosophical depiction of the society enmeshed in its own snares and webs and existing in the disgusting decadence, U.R.Anantha Murthy has shown the deadening impact of the empirical knowledge of the leader and light on his headless community. Without frequent mention and descriptions of sensual and sexual experiences, the reading of this novella would have been a nauseating experience and those descriptions seem to have been the deliberate concessions to the reader on "Buy This and Have Three Free" basis. We see that the ending resolves no conflict, no contradiction and no crisis which perplex the spiritual guru. There is no concrete solution, no answer, no consolation and no comfort except that he would unburden himself by confession.

Praneshacharya is an unfailing symbol of traditional Indian character confined to his vast store of theoretical knowledge with neither the awareness nor the ability for its pragmatic interpretation and application. So it doesn't serve the true purpose of living – happiness. It is not possible to think of the fulfillment of this purpose. That is why, he fails miserably to bring happiness to anybody—to Bhagirathi, to the community, to Naranappa, to Chandri, to Putta, to the brahmins in the temple, to Padmavati. They all seek and find happiness in their own way and show the fulfilment at their own level. Should it be presumed that a person heading a great social and intellectual responsibility with still greater spiritual and moral implications, must ensure that he is happy himself first, and not that he is confused about happiness and has no idea of what happiness is to the ordinary mortals? Their crudities and thickness must not be further thickened. All value-system is for the happiness of man and man can't be sacrificed or butchered at the altar of that. No happiness can be achieved in a state of imbalance, created and accepted without any will or strength to set it right for meaning or fruit.

A man without mobility, and if it is there, it is chained to a particular set of beliefs which constitute the very basis of all learning, cannot reach a positive resolution. And hence trouble for himself and for all those who look to him for growth, advancement and happiness. The acharya fails in his mission as a man, as a guru, as a guide, as a husband, as a friend, as a companion and as the enlightened soul. Still he is the dominating figure, the moving dynamic force of the novel! A single test, then the second test—from the dead wood into the wood, then both playing on and against each other, so fiercely, that the acharya is not out of the wood!

However, *Samskara* is a significant document in the fictional history and it is a crushing indictment of brahminism engaged in shallow practices, teaching and preaching eroticism in asceticism; scared of being exposed in the stench and stink of their libido, greed, jealousy, ignorance, cowardice and other meaner passions; their mutually exploitative leanings. Anantha Murthy is at his artistic best when he describes the discussion of this clan with the involvement of their women. These brahmins have nothing to do with the meaning and purpose of life; they are far away from *karmayoga*. The *karmaheenism* is their projected glory; their inner dissensions and divisions come to fore when they have to spend money or when they find money going out of hand. Anantha Murthy launches a sensitive and strategic battle and meets the enemy in his own field.

The realism of the novel lies in the portrait of the existential issues which dominate the daily static and stagnant life of these brahmins of the *agrahara* in Durvaspura village. Margaret Nightingale has comprehended the metaphorical significance of *Samskara* as "an Indian Journey to the End of Night". Surely, it is soul-searching; it is critical but not debasing; it is a profound answer to the tortuous question—what is above life here and hither? Those who adore themselves by creating and maintaining moral chaos in life spoil its sanctity and develop hostilities—'.ostilities against human relations; hostility against social harmony; hostility against the *samskara* of sex; hostility against the natural instincts and sanctions of human beings; hostility of the fraternity and community which can't dare. This is the passage of a rite both for the dead and the living. What else is absurdity? This is clearly visible, well-reflected, well-expressed and tastefully experienced in the lexical, literal, literary and metaphorical sense. The artist may not have any such thing in mind consciously but larger meaning and greater beauty of art emerge when the force of art works at the unconscious level. This is what appears to have happened at the hands of the creator of this exquisitely simple and daintily sumptuous and sensual delight.

9

The Death of Stagnation in Anantha Murthy's *Samskara*

The first reading of U.R. Anantha Murthy's path-breaking and path-making novel *Samskara* excited, enthralled and enchanted :ae. It had been rendered into English by A.K Ramanujan with an illuminating Afterword and well-explained all significant dialectical and linguistic terms, the close circle friend of Anantha Murthy and a celebrated poet, linguist and an intellectual of envious international standing. That is why, Ramanujan captured to the best the social, cultural and linguistic and literary ethos of *Samskara*, originally written in Kannada, in its content, style and spirit. The more I reflected on *Samskara*, the more I was lost in the unfathomable depths of the social, cultural, psychological, religious, literary, sexual, biological, mythological, autobiographical, etc., aspects of this subtle and enduring work of art, one of the most precious possessions of Indian English Fiction. Deconstruction and New Historicism or Cultural Materialism as serious approaches to its study provide good assistance in understanding greatly the strength of this novel which crosses all confines of established genres in fiction—autobiography, fiction, romance, realism, memoirs, social and metaphysical debate, controversy, a philosophical document on social history or the history of society, the travels and journeys, both physical and metaphorical, it has a dominant symbol of death; it is metafiction, let the reader, scholar or critic determine its genre.

Samskara is a lyrical narrative in brilliant prose; it is lyrically descriptive also; it is spell-binding in both respects. The well-cadenced rhythmic prose moves on to tell the tale flowing like a deep, smooth river, with the occasional ripple of waves with the uneasy disturbing foam and eddies around hiding the depths and branching off in different directions with wide and narrow expanse seeming to merge into a single whole some far away. In his Samvatsar Lecture "Five Decades of My Writing" delivered during the Festival of Letters of the Sahitya Academy in February 2007, U. R. Anantha Murthy made very interesting and fascinating revelations. He tells us that he was a doctoral student under Professor Malcolm Bradbury at the Birmingham University in U.K. where he had a week's relaxation and he wrote *Samskara* in a week. Professor Bradbury asked Anantha Murthy to reflect on one of his high school experiences and use it in his creative writings. Anantha Murthy says:

> This served as a good excuse for me for I could delay my next chapter of the thesis. Also, suddenly I remembered the story of the sleeping princess I had trickily told in the manuscript magazine. In less than a week, I wrote my novel *Samskara*.

> I must say the novel got written by me. I was fatigued having to speak English all the time, and when I sat down to write all my Kannada, alive from my childhood and boyhood memories—mostly from the whispered secrets had heard in the backyard of my house, as well as from the front yard where men sonorously recited morally ennobling Puranic stories—came back to me and the characters entered into my novel on their own. All the great, older writers in my language communicated their strength to me in a silent manner.

> (Indian Literature, *Sahitya Academy Journal*, 241, Vol. Ll, No. 5, Sept.-Oct. 2005)

Thus began the progress of the progressive novel the objective of which also Anantha Murthy desired to be progressive. The definitiveness of this immensely forceful novel soon became more evident and it asserted itself in a number of ways in the heat and dust it raised and provoked. The dynamics of the intended objective spread so irresistibly fast that the novel became a *movement*. He goes on to tell us in that lecture that a large number of renowned men of letters became his close acquaintances and that happening made *Samskara* the most happening work of art. He says:

I talked to the socialist leader Gopala Gowda about Adiga
and Gopala Gowda talked about Adiga to Kamlesh Shukla
and Lohia, and Kamlesh got me to know the late Nirmal
Verma, again a major Indian fiction writer and thinker, and
Ashok Ashok Vajpeyi, who made Bhopal our cultural
capital. Lohia talked about my novel *Samskara* to the Telgu
poet, the late Pattabhi Rama Reddy and he made it into a
film. Girish Karnad who had seen my novel in manuscript
form showed it to the painter Vasudev and Australian
Cameraman Tom Cowan and all these happenings became
a movement.

(Indian Literature, *Sahitya Academy Bi-monthly Journal*
No.241, Vol. Ll, No.5, Sept.-Oct. 2007)

These revelations made by the author himself speak abundantly
about the greatness of the novel and its outstanding stature and
status not only in the Indian English Fiction but also among the
best of the Commonwealth fiction. And U.R. Anantha Murthy was
decorated with India's highest literary award, Jnanpith in 1995.

Samskara has the sub-title as *A Rite for a Dead Man*. It has three
sections in which the story moves forward in all its grace about
which Ramanujan concludes his Afterword to the translation—
"What is suggested is a movement, not a closure. The novel ends
but does not conclude." Obviously, it is the death of the old and
the stagnant initiating the labour pains for the birth of the new.
The division of the three sections is as follows:

a) Part 1 (Chapters 1-X) deals with the issue and the crisis;

b) Part ll (Chapters 1-Vl) depicts the issue resolved, the
regeneration and rejuvenation of the spiritual head,
Praneshacharya; death of Acharya's wife; the death of
Dasacharya; the journey of Praneshacharya to self-
knowledge and self-enlightenment;

c) Part lll (Chapters 1-ll) leads Praneshacharya on his journey
and his meeting with Putta, the riddleman and the
participator; The Crown Jewel of Vedanta's meeting with
Padmavati; the show of the world and the guru's conflict
and his new dilemma.

This is the perfect structure of the novel grandly planned and
designed by a grand master story-teller. *Samskara* is a significant
document in the fictional history; it is a crushing indictment of

Brahminism engaged in shallow practices, teaching and preaching asceticism in eroticism; scared of being exposed in the stench and stink of their libido, greed, jealousy, ignorance, cowardice and meaner passions; their mutually exploitative leanings. Durgabhatta says:

> O no, a Brahmin isn't lost because he takes a low-born prostitute. Our ancestors after all came from the North—you can ask Praneshacharya if you wish-history says they cohabited with Dravidian women. Don't think I am being facetious. Think of all the people who go to the brothels of Basrur in South Kanara...

His sensual and sexual desires wake up at the sight of the widowed Chandri and his stream of consciousness flows to those ancient sages who mated with the beauties like Matsyagandhi and Maneka and even other Brahmins who married outcastes and sang of their full-blooded youth and lusty bodies. The women eyeing the gold ornaments of Chandri and cursing her.

Anantha Murthy is at his artistic best when he describes the discussion of this clan involving their women regarding the disposal of the dead Brahmin, Naranappa, who was dreaded the most by these impotent-willed practitioners of Brahminism when he was alive. Now when he is dead, he remains a dread. No one could dare check him from living a life of lust, luxury and licentiousness in open and daring violation of the accepted code of conduct. Naranappa always remained a living challenge to all these wiseacres and wiseacrees. Anantha Murthy has clearly suggested that these Brahmins have nothing to do with the meaning and purpose of life; they are far far away from *karmayoga; karmaheenism is their perfected glory*. Their inner dissensions and divisions come to the fore when they have to spend money or when they see money going out of hand. The novelist launches a sensitive and strategic battle and meets the enemy in his own ground.

The realism of the novel lies in its portrait of the existential issues which dominate the static and stagnant life of Brahmins in a colony, named agarahara, in Durvaspura village. Margaret Nightingale has comprehended the metaphorical significance of *Samskara* as "an Indian journey to the End of Night." The study of the novel cannot be confined to orthodox Hinduism, a dead, decadent and decaying value system. Anantha Murthy has shown a subtle psychological insight into the inderstanding of the social and personal predicament and dilemma; he has also depicted a crisis of civilization in which individual choice is more potent than the age-old collectively evolved and accepted code of conduct and life.

It comes out from the discussion of these malefics that even the Brahmins feel that the fulfilment of life can be achieved only in the open infringement of the established code of conduct from birth to death; that is narrower and harsher with no religious sanctions but only thrust and imposed through self-evolved and self-determined laws of social morality and spirituality. The irony is that those who practice and enforce such a code to determine the character of life in Brahminical and non-Brahminical society have neither the guts nor the strength, not even rationality, to restrain its infringement. The only considerations of such practitioners are that their monopolistic possessions must not lose their sanctity and sanctimonious sovereignty. That is why, this sacred and holy community of *agrahara* stood badly exposed when confronted by the conflict and crisis caused by the death of the only manly member of their community who lived the best and died the best. We are given to understand that any knowledge or however high our level of learning, if it lacks application in daily life and doesn't teach the art of living, is useless.

What further adds new dimensions and complicates the meaning and understanding of the thematic structure defying the finality of meaning is the lexical and metaphorical meaning of the word *samskara*. We are haunted and teased by what Aristotle asked while discussing the science of meaning—*What is the meaning of meaning?* In fact, *samskara* is so comprehensive a term that it embraces all our actions during the course of our existence in the world and even our deservingness after death. Prior to that what has been, we have no rational explanation to prove or say with certainty. However, unanswered questions remain and must be accepted as answers. Delaying answers or confusing questions is the right answer. All doubts which emerge or are raised as questions in our daily conduct, cannot be cleared. This settles our *dharma*; our ignoble actions provoked by some urgency or emergency are termed as *apaddharma*. U.R. Anantha Murthy's

Samskara is an honest and bold attempt at initiating a concrete and constructive debate to breathe new lease of life into the prevalent and predominant *Brahminism*; also at revealing and solving the enigma of Hindu society. The novella is a well-planned attack with a set strategy. The wider perspectives of the usage of *samskara* become more explicit when we learn what it means. *The Oxford English Reference Dictionary* defines *samskara* as "a purifactory ceremony or rite marking an event in one's life." It is also explained as "a mental impression, instinct or memory." *Samskara* is a Sanskrit word where it means an attempt at perfection or a preparation to become perfect. It comes to mean that our actions in daily life determine our *samskara* whether our *samskara* have the impact or shadows or even their origin in our heritage, has ever been debatable. And the debate does end but remains inconclusive. F. Kittel's *A Kannada-English Dictionary* gives various shades and layers of the meaning of *samskara*. It says that *samskara* is:

1. forming well or thoroughly, making perfect or perfecting; finishing, refining, refinement, accomplishment;
2. forming in the mind, conception, idea, notion, power of memory, faculty of recollection, the realizing of past perceptions;
3. preparation, making ready, preparation of food, etc., cooking, dressing;
4. making sacred, hallowing, consecration, dedication, consecration of a king, etc.;
5. making pure, purification, purity;
6. a sanctifying or purifactory rite or essential ceremony (enjoined on all first three classes/castes;
7. any rite or ceremony;
8. funeral obsequies.

Obviously, the word embraces the totality of our daily life in its effort to think and work for refinement, accomplishment and perfection; it is a conscious endeavour. U. R. Anantha Murthy, being himself an upper caste South Indian Brahmin brought up in conservative and orthodox family set-up, though he was fond of eavesdropping, I don't know if he is today, and a man of envious learning and erudition, seems to have used this semantic rigmarole in the story to the full. He says in his *Samvatsar Lecture*:

> Metaphors come to me as gifts when I am obsessed with a
> theme and do not know how to express it. These metaphors
> have their roots in my early rural experience but they branch
> into my adult, modern life.

After saying this, Anantha Murthy recounts an enlightening
experience of his schooldays in the traditional Samskara School.
This also adds new dimension to the meaning of the word and
the theme of the novel. We understand from the story that the
writer was seriously concerned with the putrefaction of
Brahminism that guided and governed Indian society; the
tremendous damage that its stagnant and stanching value system
was causing to the healthy growth of life. The swiftness with
which he wrote the novel and the radical impact it made at the
different levels of the intellectual life and the rapid progress it
made causing deep dents into the existing structure of
Brahminical code necessitating immediate drastic changes in its
practices and preaching and teaching, and even in the daily life
of the Brahmins themselves, leave us stunned. Therein lies the
powerful dynamics of the novel which waged a relentless epic
war, cautiously and successfully, against the rot. Many eyebrows
were raised against the novel and the writer but they failed to dim
the light on the spot. This work of art is a modern interpretation
of the age-old theme and its questionable significance and
relevance in contemporary society.

The mere issue of the disposal of the dead body of Naranappa
is lost in the din of acrimonious discussion with all its bitterness
and rancour regarding the non-issues pertaining to the
Brahminical conduct of the dead, his relationships with other
respectable Brahmins, his Brahminical status after death. The
meaner, lusty, base and lewd passions and thoughts are freely
expressed. The conduct of the great sages, Prashara and
Vishvamittar, the celibate philosopher, Shankara, Vatsyayana,
Brahmin poet, Jagannatha, etc., is recollected for their hot
passions. Mouthfuls of curses are showered on the widow, the
low-caste wife of Naranappa, Chandri, for her sexual charms and
heavy gold ornaments. We question if it is a question of rite for
a dead man or rite for all the living. The novelist deserves to be
saluted for launching missiles so tactfully that they cause a flutter
in the petticoats and *dhotis* of the well-meaning clansmen. All this
happens in the presence of the spiritual head of the community,

Praneshacharya. A.K. Ramanujan has aptly remarked, "All the battles of tradition and defiance, asceticism and sensuality, the meaning and meaninglessness of ritual, dharma as nature and law, desire (*kama*) and salvation (*moksha*), have now become internal to Praneshacharya. The arena shifts from a Hindu village community to the body and spirit of the protagonist." The stagnation and stink of learning, conduct and daily life begin to yearn for death in Praneshacharya whose delectable experience of refreshing release amidst the harmony of midnight jungle and later his journey with Putta are a pointer to the birth pangs of new in him. This is the novelist's subtle artistic venture into the lexical, philosophical, social, metaphysical, psychological and even cultural meaning of *samskara*. V.S. Naipaul says, "'Samskara' is a difficult novel...the translation is not always clear; but many of the Hindu concepts are not easy to render in English." *(India: A Wounded Civilization,* Part lll, P.P. 108-9)

The simplicity of the short narrative is subtly deceptive and elusive. Therein lies the greatness of this novel with its profound meaning. That becomes more obvious when we see how it provoked the vast scholarship and scholarly criticism, and even non-literary controversies like Mahasweta Devi's "Breast Stories." It would be a grave literary error if we read the novel as only a severe critique of orthodox Hinduism whose destiny since ages has been defined and determined and decided and guided by the prescriptive Brahminism in practice from birth till death and even after. It is not only a repudiation of the decadent, decomposing and even disgusting and deep-rooted valuesystem but, as a renowned authority on Indian writings in English, Meenakshi Mukherjee, pertinently observes,

> To read Samskara as a critique of orthodox Hinduism is to limit it severely. It is a novel worth taking notice of not simply because it repudiates a decadent value system but because it is a novel where the physical and the metaphysical fuse; where the interiority of an individual's social predicament is dealt with in its psychological complexity; where the problem-although uniquely personal—reflects also the crisis of a civilization.
>
> *(Realism and Reality—The Novel and Society in India;*
> Ch.VIII, Page-169)

It is equally astonishing that the events as well as the objects in the novel are invested with allegorical and symbolical overtones. The flowers blooming in their beauty and fragrance in the gardens of these Brahmins stand for the freshness of life and its sensual beauty and desire but these charms remain a suppressed stink in agrahara community; the words like "darkness, night, serpent, magic, lust" combine to evoke erotic effect which is a threat to the life-denying values of the agrahara. The snake has obviously sexual connotations—snake-like braids of women (Chandri's black snake-like knotted hair, Padmavati's snake-braid coming down her shoulder over her breast, even the unbraided hair of Belli has erotic associations for Sripati). This hair-serpent-eroticism runs throughout the novel. Prof. R.K. Kaul says that the alternative to Brahmin austerity is a surrender, concealed or revealed, to darkness and the demons. Chandri is an outsider, an alien, to this structured society and is also recognized by it. She is like the river Tunga the waters of which are used for multi-purposes—quenching man's thirst, washing man's filth and dirt, washing gods' images, feeding fields for man's survival. It says yes to everything. How great! So does Chandri, Naranappa or Praneshacharya or other Brahmins and their women eyeing her in their total greed and lust and libido. Meenakshi Mukherjee has found very appropriate comparison between The priest, Dimmesdale, in Hawthorne's *The Scarlet Letter* and Praneshacharya. The novel is so rich in meaning and so packed with vast immensities that it ends but doesn't conclude; its movement, and the novel as a movement, has gained momentum with greater force.

Anantha Murthy has built up the consummation of the novel in the Third Section to enhance its thematic structure by sending Praneshacharya on a journey as living experience in the company of the Riddleman Putta & Prattling Putta. It was the festival of Melige where the whole world was in tearing spirits delighting in the infinite variety of diversion and recreation symbolizing the death of the stagnation of the ennui and monotony and dullness of daily life. There was a sight of cripples as if the world was a show of cripples. Everywhere—in the crowd packed like mad, in the fair, round the chariot, around the temple—there was the confluence of the seer, the seeing and the showing. The novelist tells us:

In all this bustle and busyness, amid noises of balloons and pipes, the soda-pop and the sweetmeats, the peal of temple bells, the gorgeous spectacle of women's bangle shops, Praneshacharya walked as one entranced, following Putta. Purposeful eyes everywhere, engaged in things. His eyes, the only disengaged ones, incapable of involvement in anything. Putta was right. 'Even my meeting him here must have been destined. To fulfil my resolution, I should be capable of his involvement in living. Chandri's too is the same world. But I am neither here, nor there. I am caught in this play of opposites.

(*Samskara*, P. 115)

V. S. Naipaul says, "A recent remarkable novel, however, takes us closer to the Indian idea of the self, and without too much mystification. The novel is *Samskara*, by U.R. Anantha Murthy....Its theme is a brahmin's loss of identity...." Yes, the novel is a fine illustration of how a Brahmin loses his identity — by openly and secretly violating the age-old stinking and stagnant brahminical rites, practices and rituals and ceremonies. Naipaul further says, "Anti-brahmin feeling (and by extension, anti-Aryan, anti-northern feeling) is strong in the south...the novel as an attack on Brahmins...it shows to what extent Indians are able to accept the premises of the novel that are so difficult for an outsider: caste, pollution, the idea of the karma — given self, the anguish at the loss of caste-identity."(*India: A Wounded Civilization,* Part III, P.P.104, 109)

Thus we see that the obscurantism of the barbaric civilization, the crisis of the civilization with wide-spread stagnation and decadence, helpless and disadvantaged and in every respect, this society of men of darkness and decay, the living rot, has no answer to the present immediate dilemma. In this hour of conflict and chaos and in an attempt to resolve this all-confounded issue, the spiritual leader and learned guide with ultimate wisdom and authority, is entangled in another deep spiritual crisis. And the Acharya carries with him the burden of the immediate tension and a new experience — beyond the ever-flowing, ever-pure Tunga, in the ever-fresh and evergreen forest full of vitality, beauty, promise and soulful relief, awakens Praneshacharya to a new world, new knowledge, new understanding of sin and fall of life. He endures both these burdens at the mental, moral, intellectual and spiritual level amidst the muddle and mire of life in agrahara in Durvasapura. Beneath this is an uncommon feeling of mobility which guides him on. So he undertakes a journey which, without doubt, provides him an answer to the intensely crisis-ridden self of the Acharya. The Second Section ends with the words, "Meaning to walk, wherever his legs took him, he walked toward the east." We must remember that journey has always been a forceful symbol and adventure in the Western and Eastern literature and even in our daily life. The journey exposes the protagonist to refreshing, revitalizing, regenerating and reawakening experience for his fuller knowledge of the human world and to enable him to see how the manifestation of the divine works in it. The journey is also an enduring symbol of education, redemption, enlightenment and enrichment of life. The journey breaks the rut and gives a fresh insight into life and the pilgrim returns with a sense of fulfilment. Praneshacharya also undergoes all this transformation in his total personality. This climaxes the death of stagnation in the novel and this alone becomes a *Movement*. Anantha Murhty begins with a single test, then the second test—from the dead wood into the wood and the Acharya is not out of wood till the third test.

Obviously, Anantha Murthy's *Samskara* is a trend-setting work of art among the greatest treasures of world literature. It has fully revealed what hidden potentialities Indian writing have.

Works Cited

Murthy's, Anantha, U.R., *Samskara*, Translated with an Afterword by A. K. Ramanujan, OUP Paperbacks, New Delhi, Fifteenth Impression, 2004.

Murthy Anantha, U.R., "Samvatsar Lecture" during the Festival of Letters of the Sahitya Academi in February 2007, published in *Sahitya Academi's Bi-Monthly Journal*, "Indian Literature" 241, Sept.-Oct. 2007, Vol. Ll, No. 5.

Naipaul, V.S., *India: A Wounded Civilization*, Penguin Books, New Delhi Ed. 1977.

Mukherjee, Meenakshi, *Realism and Reality—The Novel and Society in India*, OUP Paperback, New Delhi, Fourth Impression, 2005.

10

Imtiaz Dharker—A Study in Revolt against the Prescriptive Social and Religious Sanctions

Imtiaz Dharker (1954-) lives with the passion of an undaunted rebel, not to retreat and not to fail. The intensity and eloquence of her life and poetic accomplishment have dumbfounded the male-chauvinists and have left her female counterparts in soaring spirits not only inside the Islamic social, cultural and religious setup but also outside it. That is why her life and poetry make a fascinating study in the crushing indictment of the suppressive prescriptions against the freedom, dignity and respectful living of women, especially in the Muslim society.

Imtiaz confirms our convictions that socio-cultural and socio-religious restrictions on women have robbed them of all their potentialities leaving them not only physically and mentally handicapped but also psychological wrecks age after age. The lived experiences of Imtiaz have been honestly expressed in her poetry with the courage of conviction. Her humanistic and feministic concerns with her anguish and agony, sympathy and protest give the message silently, though its deafening explosion has been felt everywhere. That is the reason that her rebellion has caused a flutter in the petticoats of the guardians of orthodox religion, custodians of culture and the pettifogging politicians. The substance, spirit and style of her daily living hold everyone to sway.

Imtiaz Dharker belongs to that generation of post-independence women poets who have given a convincing assurance that Indian English Poetry matches the best anywhere. Among these poets, we may include Kamla Das, Melanie Silgardo,

Sujata Bhatt, Eunice de Souza, Mamta Kalia, Tara Patel, etc. They have not only broadened the thematic concerns of Indian English Poetry but also shown how words and images — simple, suggestive and highly evocative — can recite the music of their anguish and agony, their irritations and humour, their observations and reflections with no sign of pretension. This serious and well-considered response to the observed and lived experiences is a drama of daily life here and there poeticized. Not only the technical excellence but also the pain and poignancy endured in suffocation and suppression have found a justifiable outlet in their creative instinct.

Indian women writing poetry is not a new phenomenon in literature. It is quite old. Eunice de Souza tells us: "Women have been writing poetry in India since about 1000 B.C. on religious and secular themes, and it is among these rather more distant ancestors that contemporary women writers are likely to find congenial voices and styles." She goes on to trace their great verse accomplishment till today. The emotion and passion and the gusto of their expression abundantly reveal what poetic power and poetic gift are in these instruments of the harmonies of nature. More abundant and fulfilling is the promise of fast increasing number of the buds and flowers and twigs arranged, displayed and placed in all their spontaneity in the bouquets of female poetic artistry and accomplishment today.

The female voice is divinely gifted with harmony and musicality if sung in creativity, not otherwise. So the orchestra of female voices is presented best with all its magic and melody when the male sensibilities are well-attuned to it. Maybe the modesty of male–chauvinism forbids the acknowledgement of their own past monopolistic gains and the present sense of their loss! Imtiaz obviously and rightly has a proud claim to be among them. The present study includes only *Purdah* group of poems, and *I Speak for the Devil* and her *Postcards from God* and *The Terrorist at My Table* have been deliberately kept out of purview for such is the demand of the present venture.

Imtiaz Dharker regards herself as a Scottish Calvinist Muslim and her poetry is a confluence of three cultures. It reflects and depicts her deeply sensitive and keenly insightful understanding and response to these three cultures. Her sincerity in handling the issues of social, cultural and religious significance sensitizes the reader equally well. The delicacy and the tenderness that run in her silky strains awakens us to the wrongs and songs of the daily life of women under the norms, rules and sanctions laid down by the patriarchal society for power dynamics. She captures even the fleeting moments and thoughts with the rare touch of the artist who is heart and soul, mind and spirit, body and intellect, integrally and indispensably associated with all that is the fragile fabric of life. The surety she gives and the impact she creates in so doing leaves the reader stunned. The exquisite simplicity of her style lends to her poems an inimitable brilliant conversation, a lively and stinging comment trapping us in the enchanting romance of *The 1000 Nights* deconstructed as a morale-booster to feminism.

Purdah has been sung and celebrated age after age in poetry, films and common parlance. With the rise of feminism and its becoming a world-wide rage, a force, purdah is seen in new light and new perspectives. We know that purdah is associated with Muslim women only, although in parts of Indian society also, even today, purdah is observed and the tradition adhered to in the same spirit of social and cultural prescription. However, purdah has greater socio-cultural and socio-religious association for Muslim women, educated or uneducated, advanced or backward, prosperous or penurious. There is an injunction to the Prophet in *The Koran* which reads as follows:

> O Prophet! Tell thy wives and thydaughters and the women of the believers to draw their cloaks close round them (When they go abroad). That will be better, that so they may be recognized and not annoyed...
>
> *(Sur Azhab)*

Obviously, Purdah was necessary in the beginning of Islam when the Arabian countries were torn by turmoil and social strife. Thus purdah ensured safety to women then and it also became a symbol of high status.

However, today, purdah is viewed as a flagrant violation of the basic rights, freedoms and dignity of women. It is treated as symbol of repression on women as it is devastatingly ruinous to the personality of women. To be covered from head to foot in the black veil is more indispensable to Muslim women. There has been and is a sporadic revolt and heated controversy in the print and electronic media against this practice to regenerate and rejuvenate female psyche. That is why its evils are viewed as outweighing its good. Imtiaz Dharker, with her social and cultural growth and lived experiences spanning three countries— Pakistan, England and India—has shown her subtle artistry in exposing the *Purdah System* in her title poems, poems related to it, in all its complexes of theme and style. The symbolism inherent in purdah also finds its subtlety and simplicity in alien cultural setting.

Purdah-I and *Purdah-II* need to be read with "Honour Killing", "Prayer", "Grace" and "Battle-line". This group of poems is packed with vast immensities. We have a fine experience of the force of courage and the force of conviction in the landscape of Imtiaz's poetry, though her poetic potentiality is no less strong in other poems. *Purdah-I* is a discreet protest and an eloquent criticism of the tradition of veil strictly sanctioned and imposed on Muslim women. Our attention is focussed on the turning point in the life of a Muslim girl when she suddenly becomes conscious of her sexual growth, others are perhaps more conscious:

> One day they said
> she was old enough to learn some shame.

And:

> Purdah is a kind of safety.
> ....
> The cloth fans out against the skin
> much like the earth that falls
> on coffins after they put the dead men in.

The conservative society, cautious and conscious, must teach her some manners, decorum and dignity for the woman in the purdah is:

> carefully carrying what we do not own:
> between the thighs, a sense of sin.

People around are the same; their looks are changed with a purpose:

> But they make different angles
> in the light, their eyes aslant,
> a little sly.

They notice her shame but purdah is a protection against undesirable, vulgar and vile looks of staring people. So Eunice de Souza regards "purdah not just as concealing garment but as state of mind." Purdah is suppressive and deadening to the intellectual awakening and growth of a woman and it is damaging to her personality. Purdah is a symbol of alienation and isolation from the outside world. It is a wall between the woman and the world. The result is that she is devoid of the first hand experience and the enlightenment this world has to offer. There is nothing refreshing in it; it curbs and restricts the speech and full expression; it is a repression of will and choice. Her mind and memory are stuffed with impressions from other women; their consciousness of sex and the feeling of sin associated with it grow to a stifle:

> Voices speak inside us.

Her plight is really miserable and evokes sympathy:

> Wherever she goes, she is always
> inching past herself,
> as if she were a clod of earth,
> and the roots as well...

And the doors opening inward and again inward reveal her seclusion. In fact, the poem is a self-examination of the *purdahnasheen* and also an honest and courageous scrutiny of other people.

In "Battle-line", Imtiaz better builds a situation depicting man-woman conflicts demarcating the boundary lines with check points and demolishing the same at will. The poetess questions:

Did you expect dignity?

The nations or the lovers or husband and wife behave the same after the battle-lines are drawn:

> when the body becomes a territory
> shifting across uneasy sheets;

> when you retreat behind
> the borderline of skin.

> Turning, turning,
> Barbed wire sinking in.

Then the whole again is at peace:

> Forgetful of hostilities
> until, in the quiet dawn,
> the next attack.

Here both the protagonists seem to have reached a tacit accord.

"Prayer" is another poem of discrimination against women. The scene is set outside the mosque where the observer, perhaps the poetess herself, is denied entry. She expresses her strong resentment against man's writ which runs large here also in the house of God and He has also yielded to man's dictate. We are told that "The place is full of worshippers", all poor; their sandals with soles, heels and thongs "forming a perfect pattern of need" are ragged and mended many times. They are thrown together in a heap:

> like a thousand prayers
> washing against the walls of God.

They appear to be the hopeful prayers of the poor. The observer is quite ironical when she questions out of sheer curiosity:

> What prayers are they whispering?

and:

> What are they whispering?

The answer to this question lies in not saying anything and the message is conveyed in wilful and tactical silence, in the subtle irony of the question itself. Imtiaz has killed many birds with no stone but the best is yet to be in her *Purdah-II* where the lioness is fiercest in her silence and kaleidoscopic depiction of the veiled Muslim women in an alien social, cultural, political and religious atmosphere. We hear the compassionate voice of the speaker but not her views. This voice forcefully expresses her serious humanistic and feministic concerns and the poetess achieves marvellous artistic success in the fulfilment of her poetic purpose.

However, another great poem, a high tragedy, deserves to be briefly discussed before this remarkably dramatic lyric. That high tragedy is "Honour Killing", the first poem in *I Speak for the Devil*. It so happened that a young woman was brutally shot dead in her lawyer's office in Lahore in 1999. None else but her family did so. It was a poignantly moving and heart-rending scene. What was her crime? She had asked for a divorce. Instead of having the heart, or for that purpose even head, to condemn the killing at any level, it was welcomed as "honour killing". Imtiaz Dharker's sensitivity could not remain dumb or mum and it burst forth in her poem "Honour Killing". It's reading makes a powerful impact and it sensitizes the reader, awakens and rouses his conscience to the urgent feminist concerns. She says:

> At last I'm taking off this coat,
> this black coat of a country
> that I swore for years was mine,
> ....
> this black veil of a faith
> that made me faithless
> to myself,
> that tied my mouth,
> gave my god a devil's face,
> and muffled my own voice.

What is left in after the easy cage of bone is squeezed and what is left out? The closing of the poem reveals greater dimensions of tragedy:

> Let's see
> what I am out here,

> making, crafting,
> plotting
> at my new geography.

The poetess understands the gravity of the situation and strongly feels that women must voice their conscience and protest against such deadening discriminations and devastating sanctions. Initially the price may be high and the tragedy too deep for tears but it is earnestly desired for the freedom and happiness of the future generations of women suffocating and rotting in such an environment. Of course, this world of dark rationality has not been the same since then. Radical sensations and thinking have set in and the emboldened spirit has started showing itself even within those confines and with considerable success. Not riddance but reformation is in sight.

Purdah-II is more elaborate, more dramatic and more eloquent in voicing the imminent concerns of lasting significance. It is a poem about many women and all merge into one. The movement of the poem reminds us of T.S. Eliot's *The Waste Land*. All these women in the poem merge into one woman; they all serve the same servitude—physical, psychological, social and cultural. Those who try to break cover with the hope and dream of a free new world face uncertainty and suffer excommunication. So the poem is an undaunted criticism of the way the society works against the freedom, dignity, will and choice of women even in alien land, here England. The tenet of the Islamic faith, "Allah-u-Akbar", comes as a reassurance and a comfort even there. The early morning call comes and the mind throws black shadows on the marble. The speaker reveals how Muslim women offer *namaaz* in a strange land. A group of 20 women hears the mechanical recitation from the hustling pages of the holy Koran without understanding a world, its meaning or sense. This is the shallowness of the traditional education with no light of knowledge. These words are nudged into the head as a pure rhythm on the tongue. They rock their bodies to this rhythm and this gives to them a sense of belonging. The 15-year–old, new Hajji who had cheeks pink with knowledge and startling blue eyes, throws a flower slyly on the book before a girl. It was the offering of the same hand with which he had prayed at Mecca. Imtiaz observes the sanctity of prayer in this sanctity of love. The impact of this incident was so powerful that it brought about a great physical and psychological change in the girl and she was unmindful of the punishment on the Doom's Day.

> you were scorched
> long before the judgement,
> by the blaze.
> Your breasts, still tiny, grew an inch.

This was a turning point in her life and her dreams were coloured with the brightest shades. A girl from Brighton, Evelyn, noticed this blooming change in her:

> I see you quite different in head.

This results in her traditional marriage. All these girls are fated to live and die with no will or choice of their own. They are "unwilling virgins" who had been taught to bind:

> their brightness tightly round,
> whatever they might wear,
> in the purdah of the mind.

This veil is not only a concealing garment but a purdah of the mind. And-

> They have all been sold and bought.

Men who appeared in their life earlier or men about whom they dreamed are thing of the past, a matter of history. These girls feel a sense of pride in them and surrendered gladly to each other's passionate delights:

> Night after virtuous night,
> You performed for them,
> They warmed your bed.

Faith alone makes up for the years of loss. They made many sacrificial ceremonies to save the man and the child and what tense and dreadful moments those were looking to and waiting for the justice of God.

> God was justice,
> Justice could be dread.

How ironical it is that these women have to observe purdah from God even!

The mood of the speaker is calm and poised throughout and the voice evokes compassion for the sorry mess in the life of these girls and women. The poetess awakens us to the degrading and dehumanizing effect of this social, cultural and religious sanction. The speaker is well-acquainted with many of such women—their past and their present. She has a round of daily meetings with them and:

> I can see behind their veils.

She can even recognize the region to which they belong before they speak. Some of these women dare and break cover, these ghosts of the girls. The speaker wants to share the experiences of these females who have been reduced to mere ghosts in such inhuman conditions.

> Tell me
> what you did when the new moon
> sliced you out of purdah,
> your body shimmering through the lies.

The speaker tells us about two girls, the swan-necked and tragic-eyed, Saleema and Naseem. Saleema had learnt from the films that the heroine was always pure and untouched. She surrenders herself to the passion of the mad old artist and wonders "at her own strange wickedness." Still there is worse in store. She gains age after losing her youth and womanhood in the continuing process of being bought and sold, annual pregnancies and marrying again. Then a revolt? Again she receives a sign of life behind the veil, finds another man and becomes another wife, begging approval from the rest. She is badly bowed under the burden of such a life.

Naseem's elopement brings shame and disgrace to the family. She is remembered among the dead at Moharram. Her encounter with the English boy brings to her a promise of freedom. Still these women behind the veil are always on their knees. Social, cultural and religious sanction and prescription this purdah is for the women in male-chauvinistic Muslim society. And how devastating it is to the female personality and psyche! Ranjit Hoskote in his *Review* published in *The Times of India* writes, "In "Purdah" she memorializes the betweenness of a traveller between cultures, exploring the dilemmas of negotiations among countries, lovers, children..." The interview of Imtiaz Dharker with Arundhati Subramaniam was published in *The Hindu* and he said, "Dharker's poetic journey is an interesting one to map. *Purdah* (1989), her first book, explored a somewhat interior politics through an exploration of the multiple resonances of the veil. The result was a work of rich texture and obliquity—of doors "opening inward and again inward," of the subtle interplay of advance and retreat across "the borderline of skin." *Purdah-I* and *Purdah-II* are marvellous modern poems of a living Indian English poetic genius who herein shows the undaunted conviction and revolt against a highly sensitive and explosive issue pertaining to the emancipation of women from a society with deep-rooted conservatism. The significance and insignificance of this social, cultural and religious prescription in the alien culture with ignominous liberal social setting has also been revealed with equal ease and poise. And Imtiaz does so on her own terms and none can dare watch the tragic drama behind and beyond the veil otherwise!

The Review of Imtiaz's Poetry in *Poetry International* observes: "With *I Speak For the Devil*, the poetry journeys further. The landscapes of the self, the metro and the country expand to embrace the world. If the starting point of *Purdah* was life behind the veil, the starting point of the new book is the strip-tease, where the claims of nationality, religion and gender are cast off, to allow an exploration of new territories, the spaces between countries, cultures and religion." Surely, here, the vision of Imtiaz is broadened into all-embracive cosmopolitanism smoothly crossing all geographical, historical, religious, cultural and social boundaries and the subject of humanitarianism has been superbly handled.

In these poems, numbering above 70, Imtiaz Dharker appears at her best. The poems in this book, even if read at a stretch, slide with the inexhaustible variety of images of the devil in all the three sections of the book, although the middle section forming the title holds the centre stage. Each piece reverberates with the message against the torn and terrifying conditions of life here and there and everywhere. The irony in the smiling welcome to the devil doesn't go unnoticed even by a casual reader of poetry which becomes a serious business later. These poems are, in fact, "a criticism of life under the conditions fixed for such a criticism by the laws of poetic truth and poetic beauty." It is not an escape from personality; it is a sound expression of personality to live full-blooded life. To be more precise and exact, these poems redefine life in the face of new potential challenges. The total emphasis of Imtiaz is on courage and conviction, honesty and humanity to fulfil the purpose of living hither.

Imtiaz is comfortably at ease and never loses her calm or disturbs her poise while she is dealing with or handling the sensitive strains of politics or poetry, purdah or pretension, virtue or virility, sexuality or sanction, grace or gaudiness. Her soul feels the torture and atrocity, agony and anguish and, then. She raves in her songs with the artistry felt only in the poetic pilgrimages of the masters. The divisions and boundaries-raised, erected and created geographically, historically, culturally, socially or religiously, by man—are looked down upon as the bogeys and ghosts of the devil in man. She wants to demolish them all so that man as man moves unrestricted and unrestrained wherever, whenever and however he likes. The message of One-God, One-World and One-Man resounds with a rare magnanimity and prophetic yearning. Her vision of cosmopolitanism haunts us with the rarity of emotional and humanistic arousal. This agony of the universal soul finds its honest expression in "Not a Muslim burial" where she devoutly wishes her body to be burnt, and not buried, so that her ashes are scattered with all her creation and its instruments mixed in it in a country she never visited. Or her body be left in a running train moving to unvisited and unseen country. How poignant is the closing of this lyric!

> No one must claim me.
> on the journey I will need
> no name, no nationality.

> Let them label the remains
> Lost property.

Devil is a lad-of-all-work; devil is a dad-of-all-work; devil is do-all; devil is woo-all. It appears that even God is helpless at the hands of the Devil. In a very little piece, "The Devil to God", we hear the devil's devilry to God:

> Dear Sir,
> I'm a fan of all your programmes,
> but the promos are bad.
> Who writes your scripts?
> Can I apply?

The devil awakens God to the bitter truth that those who serve and promote the Kingdom of God in the human world are far from being His devotees. These lines are an unsaid and unpromised assurance to The Master, "Sir", to do better justice to the implementation of his programmes. Not only this, God Himself is unaware of how the angels in His employ are misusing the divine powers and authority and all His programmes are a miscarriage in the human world. Whatever consummates in delivery is a poor miserable achievement and fulfilment. Even the devil is ashamed that how his plan or programme was misrepresented. If such are God's scriptwriters, the devil would like to apply for the job and has the sure confidence that he would do better than god's own men. Imtiaz comes to believe in "Possession" that:

> The devil is a territory
> that lets you believe you belong,
> happy when you worship
> at the mirrors.

Everywhere there are devils. They may have different forms, shapes, uniforms and figures. Those who believe that they can get rid of the devil are sadly mistaken. She says:

> Strange, the spies wear all the uniforms
> of holy men and patriots, the saffron, green,
> the smear of ash.

If you think this thing
sprouting demon wings
is planning to get off your back
you're wrong.

That is why, the devil has the honest courage to advise in "The Devil's Advice":

The bigots have better
sound-bytes.
Shut up
and eat your food.

The poetry of Imtiaz has an inimitable touch of simplicity and spontaneity in all their profundity. This lends an added force to her thought and emotion. This "spontaneous overflow of powerful feelings" is everywhere in her poetic landscape and the effortless ease with which she conveys her message creates an atmosphere of purity, freshness and innocence symbolic of nature untouched and undisturbed by the craftiness and crookedness of human civilization which has given birth to corrupt metropolitan culture with its debased social, economic, political and religious values leaving man under severe stress and strain. Devils alone are privileged licencees and we have a variety of cheats, pimps, spivs and scamsters influencing the daily working of human society. In the poems wherein the spokesman is the devil himself, Imtiaz is unsparing and relentless without losing her innocence and poise. In "The Devil's Day", she says:

The other bastard's had his day.
Now it's my turn.
Give me half a chance
And you'll see things ny way.

She also reflects on:

the small seed
of love in the wrong place.

In one of her shorter lyrics, "In Bed with the Devil", Imtiaz makes us realize the force of devil's working:

He's at it again,
making pacts for power,
hoping for a shower of goodies
if he plays it right.

The poets too sacrifice all their concern for art, society and humanity when it comes to their survival. What can be more ironical? In "The Devil to the Poet", the poet is straightforward to tell us that to play politics and to work for politics is indispensable to the existence of the poet. The poets meddle into politics whatever be their pretensions about their commitment. She says:

Don't pretend that you're
above all this,
when it comes to survival,
all your pretty words
and delicate observations
boil right down
to politics.

In "Mischief-maker", the poetess feels the haunting presence of Shaitan in front, behind, around and everywhere. It is his omnipresence that has its haloed influence on our life everywhere. In another poem, "The Location", we have a clear vision of such a presence:

The devil was in me,
walking in my feet,
living in my clothes,
owning one half
of my heartbeat.

Imtiaz finds TV no less a devil in the poem "Remote Control" that flickers to life:

called up from another plane,
moans,
takes on tongues,
tongues of angels,
tongues of devils,
tongues of men.

You can't trust anyone. It is not possible to share your secrets with anyone. Once you share your heart with anyone, you are undone. At the same time, who keeps secrets? Only devil. In "Secrets", the poetess says:

> Keeping secrets is the devil's work.
> But who shall I tell my secrets to?

People with honest and straightforward living feel worst when they have to conceal anything to themselves:

> Keeping secrets is the way
> the devil finds to eat my heart.

That is why Arshad's uncle from Bradford switched off the TV set one day while all in the family were watching it. The uncle dragged it out, smashed the screen and carted the corpse away to the dump while everybody was left dumbfounded. And the uncle was the happiest of the souls in "Dealing with the Devil" when he said:

> One devil had been dealt with,
> You have to star somewhere...

This was perhaps the daring start of Arshad's uncle to kill other devils in similar feats of encounter.

In another masterpiece, "Greater Glory", Imtiaz exposes the hypocritical and shameful conduct of man when she reveals the humiliating plight of God. She says:

> God was hijacked long ago,
> held hostage in empty churches,
> desecrated temples,
> broken mosques.

In fact, the poetess has expressed her disgust for the prescriptive religion which has taken away or brutally crushed the humanity in humans. Where is the holiness and divinity of God and where is the faith and devotion of man? The freedom, frankness and fearlessness of Imtiaz deserve an honest pat! Her gentle mock, subtle irony and rapacious raillery in the totality of human conduct on the existential level transcended into absurdity have a well-defined obligation to man as man. This man, djin-possessed, devil-enamoured and god-beleaguered, is conflict-ridden, torn-asunder, lulled and dulled by the debasing and dehumanizing socio-religious practices. And then there would be an exciting fun and festival on the Day of Judgment. "Last House Full Show" is a lively and hilarious scene in the theatre packed beyond capacity. God, the Almighty, sits in judgment with the Heads of the States and the Heads of the Governments. The entire mass of mankind, the good and the bad, the tyrants and the terrorists, yankee boys and girls, poor and the prey, powerful on the dais and the helpless sufferers in the auditorium—all are in a festival mood. Look!

> jostling into the balcony
> and the stalls, all
> the heavenly hordes with their wings
> rolled up, god up there
> eating popcorn with the VIPs,
> the devil squeezed
> into the back row with
> the bad girls and boys.

We are assured that:

> "The last judgement won't be boring."

It is not to be a documentary or a black and white:

> but your
> mis-spent life in glorious technicolour,
>
> 90mm, dolby digital
> ....

What a spectacle of "Prime Ministers dancing on top /of trains, politicians stashing /notes in bedsheets, big /women in bullet-proof capes", more and more. A huge crowd outside clamouring and begging for tickets, the black marketeers doing a roaring business. A King Kong hand could have brought about a devastating calamity but some miracle saved them all. No one waits to see the scroll of credits or discredits. People are still rushing from all corners. Suddenly the show comes to an end as:

> A breath
> begins and lifts, lifts
> us off the balcony
> into empty air, and there,
> everywhere around us, among the feet,
> the wings and floating popcorn,
> fingers unclurl, god opens
> the closed fist.

We experience that the subtle and delicate use of irony in Imtiaz is more a message than a weapon; weapon often fails, the message never, may be it takes a little longer. In "Slit", she tells us about how men keep on plotting for revenge and use callousness and cunning in the process:

> Men have a rare genius
> for revenge.
> Spare me,
> I don't know how the system works.
> ....
> Ask the men carrying
> holy books.
>
> Ask god.
> He knows.

Here some dignitary is blown to pieces by a garland so sweetly and obsequiously offered to welcome, to idolize. And the idolization was there and it shook the world. Hence this tenderly expressed concern and anguish lauding men's rare genius for revenge is known only to men carrying holy books, not holy men, and to omniscient God! We see and feel that Imtiaz expresses herself honestly and in an enviously direct manner without any sense of fear or loss. She exposes such powers, our Saviours, who decide all havoc and disaster, hullabulloo, social tensions and the daily round of life. In "Saviours", we are told:

> It's hard to say
> who's is on which side.

All the murderers are wearing
masks,
with god's face painted on.

These are highly suggestive lines about masks for men and masks for women. And they are all "the defenders of the faith."

Imtiaz feels that man is unjustly suffering when God and devil are engaged in fierce struggle to establish their supremacy and sovereignty. She suggests that it should be a war of power and pluck, politics and diplomacy, wits and hits, between God and the devil only. Let God's angels and Devil's diplomats hold conclave to avoid confrontation at any level. They have their own territories to rule. Why should man be bruised or branded, crushed or crutched in this eternal hostility? The poetess tells God and the Devil in direct terms in the poem "Lines of Control" to settle their scores once and for all and decide their own kingdoms without making man a prey to their battle of wits. She says:

If you wanted to start a fight
couldn't you just have got on with it,
the two of you, god and devil
in deadly combat
tearing at each other.......
....
but of all the battlegrounds
you could have chosen
why did you pick on me?

This is a highly symbolic poem packed with vast immensities. This short lyric brings out the maddening dilemma of man. He remains torn and tense all his life between what is good and what is bad, what is moral and what is immoral. All schools of thought have failed to help him in resolving this significant existential issue. So with all the glitter and gloom, delight and despair, pomp and paucity, prayers and pooh-poohs, absurdism is the outcome. All that man does to achieve a sense of belonging leads to alienation and isolation whether he is at the heights or at the bottom or dangling in the space like a *Trinshaku*. In such a helplessly conflicting situation, there is the glowing optimism that breeds our happiness. We can live better without thinking or doing evil to ourselves or to those who are connected with us. Shakespeare's maxim in *Hamlet* seems to offer the best solution to rid man of his tearing dilemma: "Nothing is good or bad but thinking makes it so." Farewell! you both God and the Devil. In "Guardians", we are told:

> Strange how the guardians
> of our morals
> have jellyfish mouths
> and jamun eyes.
> ....
> Odd how, in those frequent mirrors,
> Your haloes don't show up.

Then the firm resolution for salvation is daringly expressed in "In Your Face":

> In the face of adulterated gods,
> in the face of easy betrayal,
> in the face of your indifference
>
> I have assembled
> the rough materials to make
> my own salvation,
> ....
> watch
> I'm a missile
> Falling upward.

Imtiaz is poignantly concerned with the contentious issue of virtue and vice, good and bad, moral and immoral. In all honesty, she wants to rid human life, afflicted with this torn-between-the divide, of this issue so that human is comfortable with life as it comes to him and as he wants to live it ignorant of the teasing question. Freedom from this unresolved teasing dilemma would let man live untroubled and untortured by God or the devil. Everywhere on this earth, both the regents, the supremos of their respective kingdoms, and now relentlessly invading the kingdom of man, have infected, intimidated and bullied happiness. So both should retreat to their territories with their legions and leave man to himself.

   We have not seen heaven or hell and we know nothing about their existence in geography or in spaces but all religious teachings regulate our conduct here with their hope and fear. Or we know only that we have decorated these kingdoms with immortality and we are mortals here.

Even in other poems like "Being good in Glasgow", "Breeding Ground, Chicago", "All of Us", "The Djinn in Auntie", "Object", "Sofa", "They'll Say, 'She must be from Another Country'", "Announcing the Arrival.."(for Ayesha), we are made aware of the presence or the working of the devil in us or around us in a number of ways. However, the way life goes and various systems—social, political, religious—regulate and govern our life, restrict its movement, stifle its freedom, profane its dignity and corrupt what we ordinarily accept as good, virtuous and sacred. The outcome and the corollary of the myth and reality of human life are what we are all experiencing. The message which comes in dignified silence in these poems assumes utmost significance in the present day structure of life wherein the hungry wolf or the wolves are busy devising the ways and methods to reduce life to indignity and humiliation.

Imtiaz needn't search her identity or individuality. She has established both, and that too, in an abundant measure. Freedom of will and bold exercise of independent choice have been the hallmark of her daily life and she has revealed the same in her poetic accomplishment. She has demolished the religious and cultural barriers prescribed by the patriarchal society and, imposed and sometimes superimposed, upon women and endured by them. Imtiaz has awakened her fraternity to the incalculable damage done to their psyche since centuries. She has also convinced them of the triumph of the spirit in her.

However, this is not a complete triumph. She must totalize the triumph by demolishing the political and geographical boundaries also so that this world belongs to humanity undivided by man-made conventions, customs and restrictions. Such a world of freedom, of body and spirit, even after death, will be a sure guarantee for the ecstasy of the spirit for which we are divinely created. All these limitations and boundaries are an affront to God and a disgrace to the divinity of man. So life needs to be exorcised of the evil and devilish spirit of culture, religion, politics and geography. This is the world where Imtiaz wants to live and die.

There seems to be an intense yearning in her heart for the triumph of the spirit, its absence fires her spirit of rebellion, and the fire is insuppressible and unextinguishable. She doesn't belong to anyone in Sialkot, Lahore, Bombay, London, Glasgow, Delhi or Rome as she suggests and declares in unequivocal terms in her last poem "Exorcism" in the book *I Speak for the Devil*:

> I'm letting all the bad things
> fall away. I'm no one
> but myself,
> no one possesses me.

And it is like striking a petrol tank with a match stick. The closing of the poem reveals the essence of the freedom and ecstasy of the divinely created spirit when she longs for dancing, rolling, flying, rattling and clunking:

> out of a new song,
> on the move
> swirling, falling.
> This is how we belong.

In the final analysis, we may say that Imtiaz's simplicity is a spell, her lyricism is a lull, her challenge is a charm and her effort is exorcism. Her submission is her challenge; her advocacy of the devil is her soul's adventure into the devil's domain to understand the regent's governance and his indisputably faithful servants and disciples. Imtiaz may be devil's advocate but not his disciple; she may be his admirer but not her follower whereas we are all otherwise. This is our sham; this is our cant; this is our pretension; and this is our purdah—our life and living! So let's not lift it or remove it, it will decimate us all. This alone is the secret of our advancement and our very existence. The all-pervading influence of the devil, wherever we see the escape-route, it is guarded by the devil and we need be devils to cheat him to succeed only to find ourselves among the celebs of the kingdom. This is what is happening behind the veil and beyond the veil!

Works Cited

Dharker, Imtiaz, *Purdah,* Delhi: Oxford University Press, 1989.

I Speak for the Devil, New Delhi: Penguin Books,2001.

de Souza, Eunice, (ed.) *Nine Indian Women Poets*, Delhi: Oxford University Press, 1997.

Jain, Jasbir, (ed.), *Women's Writing—Text and Context*, Second Edition-2004, Jaipur and New Delhi: Rawat Publications.

Unveiling Womanhood: Dharker's "Purdah" by Rashmi Chaturvedi and *Discreet Rebellion: The Poetry of Imtiaz Dharker* by A.K.Tiwari.

11

Spectrum of Experiential Knowledge in Ramanujan's Poetry

"There is a sense of rootedness in Ramanujan's poetry, which often exists in tension with the curious and anxious sense of cultural displacement an educated post-colonial Indian sometimes feels. His involvement with Indian culture is, in all senses of the word, intimate: both deeply knowledgeable and loving; it is an involvement he allows to filter into, and enrich, his English verse."

—Ian Hamilton

How Ramanujan filters his deeper inner self in his poetry to release himself from his living and haunting tensions while working for his professional commitments in an alien culture and environment is our present concern. It may be observed in all fairness that A. K. Ramanujan is a very well-read and one of the most talented New Poets and also undoubtedly "the most gifted poet." His Symbolist-Imagist-Modern tradition of poetry has added to the illustrious legacy of Indian English Poetry, though Ramanujan occupies a countable place in British and American Poetry also. We can easily feel and understand the impact of his rich, insightful and affectionate rendezvous with the two cultures—at home and abroad—on his creativity in verse through his programmed command over his academic disciplines. Once Ramanujan wrote: *English and my discipline (linguistics and anthropology) give me my outer forms-linguistic, metrical, logical and other such ways of shaping experience and my first thirty years in India, my frequent visits and field trips, my personal and professional pre-occupations with Kannada, Tamil, the Classics and folklore give me my substance, my 'inner' forms, images and symbols. They are continuous with each other and I no longer can tell what comes from where.*

Thus the first three decades of Ramanujan's life were spent in the country of his birth with all its deep-rooted social, religious, mythological and cultural influences which profusely sensitized his mind and the reminiscences of this period remained his constant companion. Almost the last three decades were spent at Indiana and Chicago Universities in America where his astonishing intellectual growth and cultural expansion in the areas of his choice mounted his tensions. It turned out to be a conflict of convictions, cultures, and civilizations; the pain and agony of being uprooted from there and rooted here in an alien culture and environment. It was perhaps the period of the crisis of conscience and the poet in Ramanujan was at war with himself. There must be an escape-route, reconciliation and a soothing harmony to get over this social, psychological, cultural and even ethical disquietness. This intense yearning took the finest and the most glorious route wherein these tensions became creative and the severe strains of dilemma had a marvelous tranquil release in poetry. The enchanting lute tranquilized the emotions and emotionalized the tranquility in spite of frequent trips back to the native homeland. It expressed itself in artistic and aesthetic subtlety which emerged from Ramanujan's intellectual and conceptual knowledge and completely merged into his experiential knowledge. No other poet in Indian English Poetry has experienced the bliss of fulfillment from his yearning for liberation in such a situation in this manner to this extent; thus creating…*a recognizably 'Ramanujesque' world from the dailiness of the South Indian small town life populated with relations and Hindu gods.*…to use the words of Ian Hamilton. This is a spectrum of experiential knowledge created in moods and memories with a spell genuinely felt by his casual and serious readers.

This "spectrum" approach was coined by Thom Gunn, one of the most conservative and radical poets of his generation. He settled on the American West Coast, the place known for its disparate cultures and languages, but he retained his original bearings. In fact, Gunn pleaded for a "spectrum" approach to American poetry. By this, he meant the spectrum of colour, of sound and of language. Michael Schmidt elaborates it in this way: *Although remote from one another in conception and intent, the experimentalism of the L=A=N=G=U=A=G=E poets, and the inventive traditionalism of the old and new formalists, share a medium. It has rules*

that one can observe or break, rhythms one can regularize or disrupt.
Gunn's "spectrum" approach acknowledges this diversity, yet also this
inescapable commonality of resource. It can apply beyond America, to
all English-language poetries. We can approach the poetry of A. K.
Ramanujan from the point of this elaboration and lavishly delight
in its colour, sound and language. Here is the spectrum of sound,
colour and language. It may be pertinent to mention here that the
learning of the poet is so active in his creative tension that we are
consciously involved in his experiences.

We should have some acquaintance with the biographical
details of the poet's growth so that we have fair understanding
of the rich and luxurious development of his consciousness
embedded in his comprehensive knowledge of the Kannada-
Tamil languages, folklore and classics and his systematic and
disciplined studies and teaching of linguistics and anthropology
at Chicago University for about thirty years. Other profound,
liberal and notable influences that shaped up his Universal
Consciousness consistently were those of Ezra Pound, T. S. Eliot,
W. B. Yeats, William Carlos Williams, Wallace Stevens, Saussure,
Levi Strauss, Chomsky and Derrida. This information with all the
necessary details is essential to delight in the "spectrum"
approach to the study of Ramanujan's poetry. Moreover, this is
a world of his memories and reminiscences revealed to us clearly
and honestly in the poetic idiom that is ornamental to tranquilized
emotion. His elephantine memory is thickly crowded with things,
situations, relations, and events and the poet freely plays with
them to delight the reader with ironic humour and wit learning
and experience. In spite of simplicity and spontaneity, the direct
and oblique references and allusions become challenging posers.
The poet's real self is fully at work with his linguistic and cultural
studies. This is so intense, passionate and broad an experience that
it populates our own memory compartment. So delectably!
Ramanujan's superb artistry lies in his natural and groomed
ability to use words, single and compounded, as images and
metaphors and they emerge as pictures sliding before us and
opening the worlds left behind and giving a peep into its
relational significance with the modern. What a subtle union of
the antique and the modern! R. Parthasarathy has paid a glowing
tribute to Ramanujan in these words-*His poems are like the patterns*
in a kaleidoscope, and every time he turns it around one way or the other,

to observe them more closely, the results never fail to astonish. Each poem is a well-chiselled piece of beauty in which the artist has captured every minute detail showing his personal relationship with it. So these poems emerge as living pictures of Ramanujan's lived and keenly observed variety of beauty in his childhood, family, relations and society which often become his intellectual and philosophical moorings. The same seeing eye works in the alien culture also but the poet lets it work independently of homely compulsions. That is the reason that it is highly rewarding to read Ramanujan and we have this experience in very few Indian English poets.

We shall illustrate our present studies from some of the most anthologized, most read and most quoted poems from his poetry collections: *The Striders (1966); Relations (1971); Second Sight (1986) and Collected Poems (published posthumously).* It may also be noted that it is not by accident that many protagonists of his poems are women-mothers, aunts, grandmothers and cousins. His wife and father are also equally indispensable to his reminiscences. Prof. Niranjan Mohanty observes: *The poet is a caterpillar on the family tree. He lives on its leaves and finally is being eaten away by the tree.* Ramanujan's poetry concentrates on this centripetal vision and there is an excellent blending of the past and the present which creates the sound effects of multi-coloured patterns of millions of glass pieces in a kaleidoscope. According to Bruce King, "In Ramanujan's *The Striders and Relations* poetry seemed to grow out of Indian experience and sensibility with all its memories of family, local places, images, beliefs and history, while having a model in stance with its skepticism, ironies and sense of living from moment to moment in a changing world in which older values and attitudes are seen as unrealistic." In these living portrayals, we experience the warmth and closeness and the intimacy of relationships, long remembered, lost, and fresh with the staleness of living. The poet is fully alive to the surprises and the daily conflicts resulting in arguments. However, this memory rarely gives a feel of nostalgia; instead, it awakens us to his ancestral heritage which is not a tale but the truth that haunted him in the alien culture wherein he discovered and explored his real self. In such situations, many scholar-writers underwent strange predicament and the ensuing tensions turned creative. That is why, the poems of Ramanujan are the live images of "poetic beauty" and "poetic truth" and hence a lively and true "criticism of life". This is how Ramanujan's poetry amply substantiates Matthew Arnold's judgement.

In "The Striders", Ramanujan identifies his self with the New England water insect and it becomes a powerful symbol of his isolation in alienation:

"And search
for certain thin-
stemmed, bubble-eyed water-bugs,
see them perch
on dry capillary legs
weightless
on the ripple skin
of a stream.............."

The Striders, 7

His memory falls back on his sister's braids with a knot of tassel:

"But the weave of her knee-long braid has scales,
Their gleaming held by a score clean new pins."
And he is haunted by the memory of snakes.

(*The Striders*, 10).

In this very collection, we learn about a leaky tap after the wedding of his sister, his fragmented memory of "the envy of the elegant/ childless couple, and the virgin aunt........"

The poems in *Relations* have a wider spectrum of the experiential knowledge and the spaces of life as known to him and as treasured by the poet. Some of the poems here make a fascinating study in instruction and enlightenment as we see in "*Love Poem For a Wife-1*", "*Love Poem for a Wife-2*", "*Obituary*", "*Poona Train Window*", "*Still Another For a Mother*", "*Looking For a Cousin on a Swing*", "*Of Mother, Among Other Things*". Even the history poems like "*Some Indian Uses of History on a Rainy Day*" *and* "*History*" reveal the poet's past as history and his sense of history along with his large erudition. He tells us about the visit of the Fulbright Indians to the land of Egyptian wonders:

"Fulbright Indians, tiepins of ivory,
Colour cameras for eyes, stand every July

In Egypt among camels,
Faces pressed against the past....
Amazed at Pyramidfuls
Of mummies swathed in milennis
Of Calicut muslin."

(Relations, 18)

Childhood impressions also keep on rolling and ripening till they emerge as something new. The poet recalls in "History" how his "dark aunt" had been looking for something from under the cot of the just dead great grand aunt whose face was still windowed in curious unshut eyes:

"under a naked cobweb bulb
next to a yellow dim window
and my little dark aunt was there
-nose eyes and knee-bend cut
Fresh from stone for a Parvati statue-
Looking for something, half
Her body under the cot."

Family relationships in Indian English poetry form an important theme. But Ramanujan's revelation and expression is different from others and this is his epigraph for relations:

"Like a hunted deer
on a wide white
salt sand,
a flayed hide
turned inside out,
one may run,
escape.
But living
among relations
binds the feet."

Feet, no doubt, are bound but who can bind the spirit and arrest the flight of imagination? *Love Poem For a Wife* explores the experienced distance in this so-called sacred social and familial and cultural relationship with all its pain, misery, agony and endurance:

"Really what keeps us apart
at the end of years is
unshared childhood...."

At the surface level, these seem to be the trifles of memories but actually these are the trivialized essentials of husband-wife relationship wherein nothing is concealed of the one from the other and the married life supplies a soothing charm and harmony. The poet's imagination runs far and wide to trace the social and cultural beauty of this nuptial knot. We are told:

"In the transverse midnight gossip
of cousins' reunions among
brandy fumes, cashews and the Absences
of grandparents...............
and the mythology
of the seven crazy aunts."

The poem is lavishly rich wherein we see *the albums/ of family rumours*; father's noisy bath, wedding picture of father in turban, wife's innocent date with a nice Muslim friend, the drag-fight in Chicago about the position of a bathroom in their ancestral home; *the marriage of the Egyptian kings with their sisters to continue the incest/ of childhood into marriage;* and how the Hindus betroth before birth. These poems have a romance of their own. This is an environment of the alien voices of the native and the native voices of the alien.

The playful romance of childhood on a swing with a cousin leaves behind a yearning delight for which there is a life-long quest:

"When she was four or five
she sat on a village swing
and her cousin, six or seven,
sat himself against her

....
....
and we were very innocent
about it.

Now she looks for the swing
in cities with fifteen suburbs
and tries to be innocent
about it....."

—*Looking For a Cousin On a Swing*

This is not a *spontaneous overflow of powerful feelings,* as Wordsworth felt about great poetry but *emotions recollected in tranquility.* Ramanujan is a conscious artist who familiarizes the reader with his interior landscape by inscaping into it and he is direct, honest and unhesitant in his reflections.

Small-Scale Reflections on a Great House is a lyric about a great house on which the poet has small-scale reflections. He says small-scale reflections! But this is also his socio-linguistic and socio-cultural poetic artistry. He reveals two sides of this great house:

> "Sometimes I think that nothing
> that ever comes into this house
> goes out."

And:

> "And also, anything that goes out
> will come back, processed and often
> with long bills attached,......."

The poet has prepared a long interesting catalogue of *things* that come into the house and never go out; then there are those that go out and come back. The poet is pungently ironical when he says:

> "never leave the house they enter,
> like the servants, the phonographs,
> the epilepsies in the blood,
>
> sons-in-law who quite forget
> their mothers, but stay to check
> accounts or teach arithmetic to nieces,
> or the women who come as wives............"

Then the poet says:

> "Nothing stays out: daughters
> get married to short-lived idiots;
> sons who run away come back
> in grandchildren who recite Sanskrit
> to approving old men,............"

The beauty is that Ramanujan's spectrum of the social, family and cultural show leaves the reader spell-bound and gives us a feeling of satisfaction at the job having been done very well.

Before we close this spectrum show of Ramanujan's experiential knowledge, I would like to mention four more poems which give us another different view of the genius of this celebrity in Indian English poetry. And these poems also give us a different relish of his poetic dish. *Prayers to Lord Murugan* is a solemn prayer to the Dravidian God for emancipation from the literary and artistic chaos and abstractions of the modern world. The poet wants to embellish Indian classical traditions with the same sanctity as the sight of the world observed by him has shaken his sense of values. He says:

> "Deliver us O presence
> from proxies
> and absences
> from Sanskrit and mythologies
> of night and the several
> roundtable mornings
> of London and return
> the future to what
> it was."
>
> —*Relations*

He reflects on the history and philosophy of the nature of zero in *Image* as viewed and studied by the Mayans, Hindus, Jews and the Buddhists and gives his own reflections. Another poem *Self-Portrait* holds together the delights of his artistic creation with a sense of wonder marking the making of his sensibility and vision. He tells us:

> "I resemble everyone
> but myself, and sometimes see
> in shop-windows,
> ....
> the portrait of a stranger,
> date unknown
> often signed in a corner
> by my father."

Here the mood of the poet is mystical too and when we contemplate over it, it leads us into a wider world of wonder. One of the best and the finest strokes on the spectrum comes in *Another View of Grace*, a highly dramatic situation sung in a tranquil tone of the intimate passionate, surrender to the enticing and inciting blonde and how the poet failed to hold on to his sanctifying cultural values, and all controls were loosened and lost to extinguish the burning fire. The poet's honesty of integrity is revealed in all frankness when he says:

"But there She stood
upon that dusty road on a nightlit april mind
and gave me a look. Commandments crumbled
in my father's past. Her tumbled hair suddenly known
as silk in my angry hand, I shook a little
and took her behind the laws of my land."

Ramanujan's poetry thus weaves deeply meaningful patterns with effortless ease and introduces us to his spectrum of experiential knowledge that continued to grow from prior to prior and then from prior to beyond. In this respect, he has created for himself an enduring place among the poets of great and subtle artistry like Nissim Ezekiel, Keki N. Daruwalla, Shiv K. Kumar, Jayanta Mahapatra, Kamla Das, A.K. Mehrotra, R. Parthasarathy, Gieve Patel etc. It is Ramanujan's poetic technique which immediately attracts the attention of the reader and lends new strength to his poetry. According to Bruce King: *His poetry blends the techniques and conventions of European, Indian, American and British literatures, with those of Kannada, Tamil and Sanskrit......The conciseness of his images and the way his tone sometimes seems distant and unrevealing may be as much influenced by the conventions of classical Tamil as by modern imagism.*" Sometimes it happens naturally out of his deep-rooted knowledge and experience of the classics, linguistics, anthropology and culture and civilization; but largely these become the compulsions of his serious and conscious attempt in great verse. Prof. Rama Nair also shows his remarkable talent in her scholarly studies when she observes: *Images play a decisive role in Ramanujan's poetry. It is through them that he communicates his ideas. An image in his poem is used graphically to elaborate a particular thought. The skilled use of metaphors is another proof of Ramanujan's superb craftsmanship.*"

The technique emerges and evolves to cope with the content which is both the obligation and compulsion of the artist in the poet. This is what will remain the lasting fascination of Ramanujan's poetry!

Works Cited

Gokak, V.K. (ed.), *The Golden Treasury of Indo-Anglian Poetry (1828-1965)*, Sahitya Academy, Delhi, 1989.

Hamilton, Ian, (ed.), *Oxford Companion to 20th Century Poetry*, OUP, New York, 1996.

King, Bruce, *Modern Indian Poetry in English*, OUP, Delhi, 1987.

Parthasarathy, R, *Ten Twentieth Century Indian Poets*, OUP, Delhi, 1983.

Nair, Rama, *The Poetry and Translation of A. K. Ramanujan*, Prestige Books, 2004.

Sahu, Nandini, *Recollection as Redemption*, Authorspress, New Delhi, 2004.

Schmidt, Michael, (ed.), *The Harvill Book of Twentieth Century Poetry in English*, Rupa & Co, New Delhi, 2000.

12

A Butterfly Rides the Winds—
The Mind and Art of Dr. Rita Malhotra

The title must not be misconstrued in any way even by the remote stretch of imagination. My association with Dr. Rita Malhotra, a mathematician-poet, is very recent and I have found her prolific and abundant, very interesting to converse with on a variety of subjects, notwithstanding her shakiness in her ventures and frequently undervaluing herself, perhaps the modesty of the fair sex. When evaluated fairly, her shakiness also appears to be a significant part of her envious level of proficiency, both as a teacher and a poet. Her creativity in poetry and her zealous participation in national and international poetry conferences, workshops and seminars have earned for her many laurels and have also added some feathers in her cap, if she wears it. Her poems have been translated into Spanish, French, Chinese, etc., and they adore some reputed poetry anthologies also. Needless to say that her position among great pre-colonial and post-colonial Indian English poets like Sarojini Naidu, Toru Dutt, Kamla Das, Melanie Silgardo, Mamta Kalia, Eunice De Souza, Imtiaz Dharker, Sujata Bhatt, etc., is secure.

After reading her book, *I am not your woman and other poems,* I could not help reaching the conclusion. I found Rita touching upon the stark and stinking social realities, pleasant and refreshingly perfumed and coloured love, passion, sex in memories, imprints and imagination perhaps and also observation. The rich and diverse variety of images becoming symbols and metaphors, simple and complex; her conscious use of small letters everywhere with absolutely negligible exceptions, lend unique force to her themes and stylistic devices and rhythmic tunes and tones. All poems are compact, compressed and short memorable lyrical pieces. I couldn't decide easily on what aspect of Dr. Rita's poetic accomplishment I should write till I remembered her poem, "Silence", (p64) which I found a poem of well-rehearsed parade of spontaneous reflections on the rhythm of dancing hues and fragrances, movements and sounds of all rich loveliness of creation. What a symphony of the spoils of moods, human and divine, authenticating the sanctity of LIFE! She says:

> ....
> in the mirror of my eyes
> beaming carnations
> a riot of magic hues
> roses blush wild as
> the sea of red reflects
> beautiful perfection
> verdant blades in gentle sway
> gold-winged butterflies
> ride the winds...
>
> ("Silence", p. 64)

Again "Borrowed Bliss", simple, spontaneous and symphonic, is the poem of flights of a butterfly riding high on the highs, secure and ecstatic, viewing and reviewing, unscared and assured all the time. Its wings flap "above the ochre slopes", "over desert hills","over verdant forest pines" and then:

> I race past wayward winds
> to join the night in revelry
> I sway in a million golden shades....
> ....
> I commune with divinity
> then fly back home
> ....
> into time's open arms
> into open dreams
> with a share of borrowed bliss.
>
> ("Borrowed Bliss", p. 58)

Thus the butterfly rides and rides into time and space, into dreams and desires, into society and its malaise, unrestrained and as long as she likes. It is from here that the poetry of Rita Malhotra is born, emerges or emanates. There is "The sea within" (p. 65) which tells us about the poetry of interior landscape, interiorized to exteriorize her disturbed fathom. Rita's concept of poetry is further clear when we read "Poem" and "Poems" (p.p. 89 & 90). We learn that life is a disfigured poem with "the space between lines" and "the blanks between words" and these sing of love from where the ashes have been blown; blurred and bruised thoughts reject and abandon the pains of daily existence. However, as Rita tramples upon dry leaves and dead flowers, her emotions, delights, pains, concerns and reason express themselves in the incessant process of poetry. She says:

> then fresh words appear
> fresh desires grow
> poems flow.
>
> ("Poem", p. 89)

Such a wonderful commencement of the process of Rita's poetic creation reminds us of William Blake's Introduction to Songs of Innocence when we read Rita's "Poems". Her range of poetry moves from the wealth and beauty of nature to the waste and barbarity of the nuclear age. Rita says:

> I plucked a poem
> from the poetry tree
> draped in rainbow hues,
>
> ....
> I reached for the second
> that ran in feline leaps
>
> ....
> the next one watched
> snow-peaked heights
>
> ....
> so went on a poem-filled trek
> through nature's lavish bounty
>
> ....
> sad lines echoed agony
> spoke of monster-man
> of nuclear war and ghoulish death,
> of shells landing on bamboo groves
>
> ....
> Chaos tore the heart.
>
> ("Poems", p. 90)

That is how I thought of assigning this title to the article. This furthers my interest in studying the mind and art of Dr. Rita Malhotra. Her interest in poetic compositions is so ardent that sometimes I wonder how she finds time to fulfil her other personal and professional responsibilities and obligations. Dr. Rita has prodigious energy and enthusiasm to accomplish herself in whatever she chooses to take up. I have noticed that she has a strong urge to create challenging tasks and situations for herself and meets them with equal dignity, grace and success.

Some persons have the rare gift of crossing the boundaries of their chosen field and venture into another pursuit and that pursuit becomes their first love, though they honour their commitments to the chosen field also with unflagging zeal. The abilities and capabilities of such persons are further sharpened and these get a strong boost. Then the pursuit overshadows, if not eclipses, the chosen field. When these two strains are incompatible and the person concerned strains every nerve to reconcile the recalcitrant opposites, it consciously takes a heavy toll on the total personality. But unswerving resolve to pull through to push the pursuit to the pinnacles where the fresh glow of the each ray of the new dawn everyday welcomes and embraces the pilgrim when the fatigued pilgrim sits aplomb to relax and look back at the steep paths trodden with the abundant load of appreciation, praise and reward. Such a person is genius redefined leading the arts, pursuits and professions to the new horizons.

Dr. Rita Malhotra scrambling for quite long against the odds and obligations of her life, profession and pursuit to show to the world that life has a concrete meaning, a noble purpose, charming dream, transcending vision and, above all, an aura of accomplishment. All lies compact before us in her ability to create and cope with challenges and to defeat them and still embracing them. This is done with the accuracy and exactness of mathematical calculations and certainties well observed, sensitively guzzled and artistically defined in her poetic creations. She says:

> we versify life
> Bathed in its beautiful sufferings.

> ("Images", p. 65)

Where:

> kaleidoscope of dreams afloat,
> Folded hands gently urge
> "solitude" forsake me not.
>
> ("Silence", p. 64)

And also:

> the sea within churns
> Frenzied foam-lined waves soar
> Shivering, trembling.
> The sea within (p. 65)

Yes, the poetry and the profession of Rita and also whatever she professes is "the sea within" which keeps on churning ever to whip up soaring, shivering and trembling frenzied foam-lined waves in their crystalline settlements on the vast infinite shores of her poetic activity. It is impressive splendid parade of the numberless small segments of a huge army out to celebrate the triumph of effort over ennui and existence. She says:

> she is victorious
> yet defeated.
>
> ("Masks", p. 67)

> to map the tomorrows
> in fresh garden-green
> optimism.
>
> ("Memory Map", p. 66)

Dr. Rita is invincible in her impressions when she enjoys the delicacies of the lavish feast of life:

> I can feel the earth open wings
> I feel the skies touch ground.
>
> ("Feast", p. 68)

Rita assures us that life can be and will be a lavish feast only if it is cradled in Cupid's arms; the trance is more lavish in such a mood. At the same time, her agony flutters her soul in "Orphan" (p.. 68). This is a poem of heart-felt concern, sympathy and worry which reveals the poet's ever-alive humanity. The girl-child, an orphan— "a frost-bitten flower" — is ready to plunge into her "turmoiled tomorrows". It is highly suggestive and evocative. She expresses herself frankly and honestly and without any inhibition. This is a great quality of the artist and Rita boldly shares what she feels is the truth or the everyday reality.

What strikes the reader the most in Rita's poetic endeavours is her painful concern for the wrongs and crimes inflicted on children, especially girls, and women whatever be their status. Her attitude in this respect is sociological and humanistic. She is sensitive to the insensitivities of society against them in its delights in sexual exploitation, selling women in marriage or otherwise, child abuse, tragic plight of widows, etc. The poet in Rita wakes up to a mission to threaten such a society with exposure and excoriating indictment. In most of her poems on this theme, we encounter situations which depict debasing and disgusting social realities in a variety of images to rouse the slumbering conscience of our daily world delighting in such wrongs and crimes and goes scot-free to mock at efforts and sanctions. In "Child Rape", she portrays the rape of a child of seven staying home to look after the toddler while the parents were out to fight their battle of survival. Only a week ago, she had been admitted to school:

> to be distanced from
> the indignity of existence...
>
> ("Child Rape", p. 100)

Today, corpse's clothing draped her white uniform the sight of which maddened the helpless mother whose laughter:

> echoes like strings of an instrument gone wild.

Dr. Rita, in a remarkably controlled emotion, tells that-

> injuries of time continue to be inflicted
> claws of a diseased society continue to
> advance, engulf and haunt.

The last three words heighten and emphasize the tragedy that occurs day in and day out engulfing the prey in its pain and agony, slur and stigma, torment and haunting all the time to come. What deepens the tragic tension is that such situations are unstopped and unstoppable. Rita's message is clear and loud and even the clogged ears open to hear its cry and shriek.

In "Dawn", she says with still deeper concern and greater anguish:

> she dies everyday
> broken columns of thoughts
> bleed memories
> time advances, reason returns...
>
> ("Dawn", p. 98)

Rita's poems are pictures painted still and which become movies in readers' minds. Sometimes they look to be the picture story tests to the readers as candidates to jolt their unconsciously ignored or hidden or consciously concealed sensibilities. Children are sacrificed at the altar of gods; they suffer such atrocity where in the chaotic clanging of temple bells, we hear the prayer of a girl child. In "Earthquake Images", this child:

> is devoured alive
> to the will of gods.

And:

> in tearful frenzy she digs
> into the ruins of a home that was
> to flush out memories, if not lives...
>
> ("Earthquake Images", p. 96)

Rita's concern for the indignities and inhumanities inflicted on girl children and widows are more conspicuous than her treatment of love, passion and beauty. Her own response is heart-rending and poignant, emotive and rhetorical, compassionate and captivating. She is quite emphatic in her revelations and, while doing so, her abundant use of the wealth of similes and metaphors turns out to be a force to reckon with. Girls are sold in marriage and their plight is rarely realized but Rita exposes the unabashed acts of people who are the shame of society without their realizing it. Rita says:

virginity huddled in surrender
she is a fragile bloom, fresh
in a dark cellar.

("Sold", p. 41)

Her marital happiness lost its glow and fragrance in the stinking
and detestable, false and shallow, adoring preparations and the
sharply contrasted surroundings wherein we hear her-"hapless
screams" and become a living witness to:

she had just lived her first death.

("Sold", p. 41)

Dr. Rita is ironical and sarcastic to awaken the reader that in a
country or society which makes tall declarations and professions
regarding its high adorations and honour given to women, this
is the most dehumanizing treatment given in reality. This is a
daring exposition of the society with a double face and double
standards. *Dr. Lee Kuei-shien, a Taiwanese Poet says,* "Dr. Malhotra
is very sensitive in poetic imagination with a certain abstract
thinking in combination with deep concern about social reality."

In "Cookie—woman", Dr. Rita acquaintances us with one of
her master strokes when she uses stark, violent images and
metaphors to design a woman's most pitiable and most miserable
condition. Man is a master-baker whose "chocolate and raisin-
studded" shapeless mass is shaped by "the oven's volcanic fury."
And:

woman, born, reborn
and born again
all in one birth
a function of man's desire.
....
relished bite by bite until
dream defeated,
she is a shapeless mass once more.

Man obviously treats woman only as an instrument of sexual lust
and she is rendered hollow inside out. This deterioration of her
charm and beauty into a horrifying and deadening lump of flesh
with no freshness leaves her a psychological wreck wrecked into

a living death. She tries to rejuvenate her lost glamour by external aids and flattering comments of hungry man but fractured forties can't be shaped into angelic fourteen and she becomes a "sour-bellied whore", to use a Shakespearean expression. I wrote "Mangled Wits" on a similar theme:

> Man misguides me into doles
> And the illusion of model roles.
> Flooded with fairy thoughts
> My head swims.
> Tortures and disgraces
> Shadow and haunt me.
> My idolized image taunts me...
>
> ("Mangled Wits", p.10 in *Rustling Leaves*)

"Woman" is the biographical sketch of a woman, her life of struggle, fierce and ferocious, like a river assuming countless shades and shapes with fickle twists and turns:

> ravages of time ignored,
> she advances, relentless
> a swelling surging ripening tide...
>
> to: expand into an ocean
> liquid arms extended
> in welcome embrace
> to prayers, sins, ashes and all.
>
> ("Woman", p. 36)

This is the psychological and physical, emotional and eternally tender behaviour of a woman in goddesses and a goddess in woman. Rita's feministic concerns and sympathies bear a stamp of authenticity and genuineness. That is what assures her a place beside the eloquent proponents of the cause of respect, freedom and dignity of woman from birth to the end of her life. Although she has not fixed the responsibility for such a sorry mess on any one or system, yet it is obvious that the paramount position of man and the resultant male-chauvinism are squarely to be blamed. What hurts us more is not the hurts and bruises he inflicts on woman but his delight and his Mephistophilian mock while so doing and after the damage with no sense of remorse. Perhaps that is the reason that we all and the law are the mute spectators to ever-rising graph of such wrongs and crimes in the land of Savitari and Sita, Durga, Lakshmi and Saraswati, Kali, etc.

In "Mirror", Rita uses a more brutal image to depict a woman's position

> she is a mere cog
> in the wheel of repression.
>
> ("Mirror", p.84)

And in "Brothel Queen", she looks at this atrocity from another angle "angel of darkness":

> ambushed by illicit desires
> men, who move from
> the powerless wife
> to the powerful prostitute....
> she is my defeated self.
>
> ("Brothel Queen", p. 71)

In "Unwed Mother", Rita portrays another sadder side of a woman's life whose:

> hurt never lasts
> grief never lasts
> only memories do.
>
> ("Unwed Mother", p.30)

We read more poems on these burning issues pertaining to the actual status of women in our society that adore millions of pages in literature, sociology, law, womanology and feministic studies, may be to enjoy *woh wah* and to be in the swim, but Rita doesn't seem to have any such intentions. Her soul-stirring message is conveyed in "Child Prostitute" (p.16), "Child Bride" (p. 23), "Widow" (p. 59) etc. are more devastating in this respect. *Widow* is a painful and poignant poem of the tragic plight of a widow helplessly trapped in the messy and sticky religious corruption where:

> unholiness emanates from
> the holy city of pilgrimage and prayers.
>
> ("Widow", p.59)

She helplessly endures the feasting "animal eyes" of the vultures around and feeding them with "her sadness-nest". The poem is full of live images richly wrapped in right and appropriate words invested with meanings that are a soulful delight of poetry. Child prostitution is a social evil, a crime, a slur on the guardian angels of society, an economic necessity that work at delicacy and decency. "Child Prostitute" is marked by artistic bluntness, naked images, helpless surrender to inhuman and detestable exploitation in utter social and moral degradation. The poem is a protest and also a high-sounding appeal to the slumberous conscience of society that happily allows it. In "Child Bride", Rita's artistry is at work more artistically. The title elaborates the situation in a straightforward manner wherein she tells us about life without love, passion without love, desire without love, marriage without love; all love hinges on "the pungent smell/ of loveless desire" where "the music of/her kaleidoscopic glass bangles" breaks into the ruin of thousand coloured fragments and remnants. Rita deserves to be decorated for espousing and relentlessly taking up the cause of feminism, femininity and womaninity.

If Rita has an enduring passion for justice to women in all walks of life so that they also feel that they are an indispensable and integral part of the evolution in this New Age, she is not without passions that are elemental and essential to feel life, fulfill life and initiate the dawn of happiness to enthuse the environment with brightness. Such poems are also her "spontaneous overflow of powerful feelings" and rarely "emotions recollected in tranquility". Perhaps she can't escape from her personality and to design "poetic truth" and "poetic beauty", she knows that poetry has to be "a turning loose of emotions" also. Sometimes. In "Love", a poem of:

> reckless passion on rampage
> the raving flames are red
> as we make love

("Love", p.17)

> because: I am the proud canvas
> on his easel
> splashed in rainbow hues
> of his proximity

("Love", p.17)

"One" is a short, simple lyric of deep passion wherein the poetess feels:

> you are happiness
> you are love
> inseparable, you and I...
>
> ("One", p. 28)

and in very fine, ornate and reflective metaphors, great signs of her poetic maturity, inspite of the "green minds", Rita says:

> let dark green minds
> dark as deep wells
> sing their hate songs
> we shall hum only anthems.
>
> ("One", p. 28)

What an artistic linguistic twist! A reminder of Frost's "Stopping By Woods." Even Peter Thabit Jones, Editor, the Seventh Quarry, Wales, U.K. has observed, "Malhotra's poems, often compact, display what the American poet Robert Frost referred to as "a careful casualness." It is through her poetic voice, honest, delicate, intelligent, individual yet universal that arrests the reader and leaves him or her with something truly profound and lasting."

"Storm", a well-conceived short and tender love lyric, is suggestive and evocative; the very title itself is a poem. It does raise a storm in the tranquil hearts:

> love trembles
> breasts burn with
> autumnal passion
> seraphic glow on lily face.
> and
> fragrance of a promise
> fills the air
> as carnations open petals.
>
> ("Storm", p. 29)

These are highly sensual images which hold a powerful appeal to the eye, ear, sight and smell without any oblique reference. Similarly, after storm, there is "Tempest" in which:

> the mirror co-operates
> as she stands disrobed
> wearing only his love...
>
> ("Tempest", p. 45)

After this, what happens is a delectable experience when body and soul meet and unite and achieve the trance of heavens:

> night traverses the highway of rapture
> stars linger to let love fulfil itself
> then reluctantly grew dim
> the song of dawn
> sings a lullaby to them
>
> ("Tempest", p. 45)

> Browning says in "The Last Ride Together":
> Earth being so good, would heaven seem best?

Yes, when the stars also grow dim, though in utmost reluctance, the fresh song of dawn sings a lullaby to the lovers rolling in the ultimate bliss. Well done, Rita! Only Keats could create it to the level of consummation! In "Kiss", Dr. Rita tells us about the miracle of kiss in completely overwhelming bliss. There is no need for preparation; it is the first kiss is highly inflammable. Of course, the firsts in life have charming memories, even beyond the grave. The short, delicate and violent lyric has a direct and dramatic opening-

> the first kiss sets them ablaze
> ....
> two enslaved bodies
> passion chained
> one wild rhythm
> the flood of fire surges
> through numerous mystery-bonds
> untamed, unashamed.
>
> ("Kiss", p. 52)

The next stanza is meant seriously to be enjoyed and experienced otherwise don't read it! This reminds us of Keats' Ode to Psyche and "Eve of St. Agnes". These emotional stirrings and passionate arousals must throw us into "unbridled ripples of ecstasy" till the flame ebbs in "the ocean of dark damp desire" and "Cupid's eyes fall in deep sleep." After reading Rita's protests against crimes against children, women and widows and appeals for social respect, dignity and freedom untroubled and unmarred by advances and overtures, when we read her love songs and lyrics to be sung and relived, we are oblivious of what the hell goes around and these lyrics mesmerize the reader and also disturb to the very essence.

Other mild doses in different ways can be had in "Plea", "Picture Perfect", "I am not your woman", "Desire", "I do not smell of dead flowers", "Funeral", "House and Home", "Void", "Cyber-Love", "Feast", "Ameena", "Belonging", "Wine-sweet", etc. Dr. Rita Malhotra plays different tunes on the instrument of love like Spenser, Donne, Shelley, Keats, Tennyson, Christina Rossetti, Morris, Lawrence and Yeats. However, her love lyrics are short enough to reveal the subject and she is unconventional in her treatment, images, metaphors and devices. At first reading, one may not be prepared to believe that Rita is a love poet of this stature. Ruth Wildes Schuler, Editor, Prophetic Voices, U.S.A. has rightly said, "Rita Malhotra's poetry explodes with passion and beauty. Even the darkest despair lightens under the magic of her pen. Metaphors dance through raging storms and sunsets to quicken the reader's heart. Here is an unforgettable poet."

Dr. Rita, like the American poet, E.E. Cummings, seems determined not to use capital letters in her poems. May be the titles of the poems and the use of 'I' are the sole exceptions. I told her once to remove these exceptions totally from her poems. She thought that my simple suggestion was deceptive. But I convinced her in all honesty. Hopefully she remembers. Even if she doesn't, she has ensured for herself a place among the immortals of Indian English Poetry and can be indisputably ranked among the moderns of the moderns in her rationale, spirit and content and device of poetry. Some greater than herself have been genuinely inspired to translate her poems into French, Chinese, Spanish, etc. and she deservingly is an honorable guest at national and international poetry festivals, workshops, seminars, and even, poetry lectures and evenings. How does she have such a poetic strength to endure that much load with all the mathematics around? A lavish poetic play of life's mathematics with everyday realities!

Works Cited

Arnold, Matthew, *Wordsworth in Essays in Criticism.*

Bhushan, R. K., *Rustling Leaves;* Authorspress, New Delhi, 2008.

Eliot, T.S., *Tradition and Individual Talent.*

Malhotra, Rita, *I am not your woman and other poems,* Sampark, New Delhi, 2007, (Text and opinions quoted at the back cover of this edition.)

Wordsworth, William, *Preface to Lyrical Ballads.*

Thorn in the Flesh of Man-Woman Relationship, Sex and Love: A Study of R.C. Shukla's *The Parrot Shrieks*

The treatment of love and sex in the poetry of all languages, art, painting and sculpture has always been a charming fascination. So has been the sweet temptation and irresistible desire to read and enjoy the same to beyond the last dregs. The treatment and studies of the subject have always faced a challenging crisis— social, moral, psychological, legal and even biological. However, with the radical growth of consciousness, there has been an astonishing change in our attitude to sex and love as poets, critics, artists and the common mass of mankind today, though we still adore and idolize the same with indecency, vulgarity, obscenity and even pornography. This aspect of our daily existence and life has never lost its sheen, luster and even glow, in determining, sustaining, sublimating and destroying the very quintessence of man-woman relationship.

The wealth of the history of the subject is not only profoundly rich and abundant but also ever-fresh and ever-stimulating like the dense forest with all its vegetation, eternal inexhaustible springs gushing forward into brooks, streams and rivers surviving with the ferocious and the submissive inhabitants. It would be an unpardonable injustice if I mention some stalwarts and unmention many, many sages, saints, prophets, poets and artists of the genre. However, the literary obligations indispensably require some citations.

D.H. Lawrence is highly idolized as the greatest sage and saint of the poetry of love and sex today. His novels, stories, plays, poems and the bulk of critical essays incessantly enlarge upon the issues related to this life-force. Since the present study pertains to the three volumes of Dr. R.C. Shukla's *The Parrot Shrieks*, I would like to quote from some poems of D. H. Lawrence. He says:

> The body of itself is clean, but the caged mind
> is a sewer inside, it pollutes, O it pollutes
> the guts and the stones and the womb, rots them down,
>   leaves a rind
> of maquillage and pose and malice to shame the brutes.
>   ("Obscenity", p. 463)

> Sex isn't sin, ah no! sex isn't sin,
> nor is it dirty, nor until the dirty mind pokes in.

> We shall do as we like, sin is obsolete, the young assert.
> Sin is obsolete, sin is obsolete, but not so dirt.
>   ("Sex isn't Sin", p. 463)

> Leave sex alone, leave sex alone, let it die right away,
> let it die right away, till it rises of itself again.
>   ("Leave Sex Alone", p. 471)

> O pillars of flame by night, O my young men
> spinning and dancing like flamey fire-spouts in the dark
> ahead of the multitude!
>   ("Spiral Flame", p. 439)

> When modern people see the carnal body dauntless and
> flickering gay
> playing among the elements neatly, beyond competition
> and displaying no personality,
> modern people are depressed.
>   ("When I Went to the Circus", p. 445)

> Women don't want wistful
> mushy, pathetic young men
> ....

> Mushy and treacherous, tiny
> Peterlets, Georgelets, Hamlets,
> Tomlets, Dicklets, Harrylets, whiney
> Jimlets and self-sorry Samlets.
> ....

Women want fighters, fighters
and the fighting cock.
....
The fighting cock, the fighting cock-
have you got one, little blighters?
Let it crow them, like one o'clock!
                ("Women want Fighters for thier Lovers", p. 457)

Come not with kisses
not with caresses
of hands and lips and murmurings;

come with a hiss of wings
and sea-touch tip of a beak
and treading of wet, webbed, wave-working feet
into the marsh-soft belly.
                                        ("Leda", p. 436)

We've made a great mess of love
since we made an ideal of it.
....
It is not love any more, it's just a mess.
And we've made a great mess of love, mind-perverted, will-
perverted, ego-perverted love.
                                ("The Mess of Love", p. 472)

We may continue from the treasures of D.H. Lawrence to listen
to the shriek/s of Shukla's parrot but the limitations demand a
reluctant stop and be happy with the approach, application and
attitude that emerge out of these precious gems. This acquaints
us intimately with sex and love in their sacredness and sanctity,
sinfulness, voluptuousness and vulgarity, necessity, need,
comfort, consolation, relief, escape, etc.,— physically, mentally,
psychologically, intellectually, morally, socially; again etc.
Obviously, love and sex are eternally present thorn in our flesh;
its discussion is thornier than the topic; it is thorniest when treated
as a taboo and we feel shy or suppressed to talk or speak about
it; it is shameful and degrading and debasing when we come out
with pretensions about it.

R.C. Shukla's *The Parrot Shrieks* (3 Vols.) is at its best in taking
the thorn out and when it is being taken out, it causes pain but
when out, it is a heaven of relief when the shriek softens but

doesn't end. I don't think any other Indian English Poet has done so with such candidness, chivalry, directness and dare and while reading these volumes, we feel the personalized experiences of the poet universalized. Thanks to the glory of the Muses! Also it astounded me to think, with due apology to Dr. Shukla, if he has done anything else than to be licentious with Lauras, Biches, Fornarinas, Juliets, Rosalinds, Violas, Cleopatras, Doyles, Harriets, Fannys, Maud Gonnes, Dianas, etc. D.H. Lawrence records the cry of chastity "in this mind-mischievous age!" when he says:

> O leave me clean from mental fingering
> from the cold copulation of the will,
> from all the white, self-conscious lechery
> the modern mind calls love!
> ....
> From all the mental poetry
> of deliberate love-making,...
>
> ("Chastity", p. 469)

Today sex is in the mind and love is nowhere, not even in sermons and obsequious reverence. To be more plain, or for that matter, blunt, all love is in sex from where flows all goodness, nicety, decency, charity, virtue, nobility; and without it, the indispensably essential basis of the working of our life, smooth and harmonious man-woman relationship, remains disturbed, perverse, strained and stagnant. In his Prefatory Note to the first volume of *The Parrot Shrieks*, R.C. Shukla says with forthright honesty of purpose:

> The poems included in this volume are poems about love between a man and a woman, an exercise in which the latter is normally passive and secretive. The woman's love consists in her accepting the advances and then receiving whatever is given to her in the name of love. These poems are a very scrupulous expression of what I have myself seen around me. I must say, the poems that are here are a very unpretentious consequence of my own observation of the drama of love.

In these lines, *around me* and *my own observation* need some particular attention. Then in his Preface to the third volume, he says:

This is the third part of my trilogy *The Parrot Shrieks* delineating the vagaries of man-woman relationship. Although I do not have a viable faith in what is commonly known as romantic love, I have written a large number of poems on this subject chiefly to explore myself. I have glorified love as I have repudiated it in my poems....In love, it is the man who gives, the woman only receives. The conflict arises when the man envisages his woman to be a giver.

This amplifies his approach and attitude to love and sex in this matter though he considers love the light of hope dimmed and extinguished by disbelief bringing despair. He further states that in love,"loyalty is a capricious liability conditioned by so many upheavals."

Good are the times and fortunate is Shukla that he is free from the wrath of the censorious and safe from the cruel obscure allegations of being nakedly sensual and perverse or being sex-starved in his poetic portrait. It is a poetry of the pleasures of romantic agony or even the yearnings for that or even the wasting influence of misplaced love in *La Belle Dame Sans Merci* or Dantes's *Bice* or Shelleys's *Harriet* or Keats's *Fanny Brawne* or Tolstoy's *Anna Karenina*, Yeats's *Maud Gonne*. As we move on to read these poems from the first to the last, we are sweetly reconciled with the erotica and exotica of *femme fatale* in her complete localization by R.C. Shukla. Even after we are done with these volumes, we feel that notwithstanding the exhaustiveness of the exposition of the delicately disturbing subject, there should be more frank additions to our catalogue. Such is the ageless freshness and lavishly rich fertility of love and sex in determining and guiding the daily course of the sweet, sour salt and bitter of man-woman relationship in mythology, literature, painting, sculpture, painting, music and everyday life everywhere since antiquity. We are ever-fervent in sucking the most out of it whatever be our art or mode. The poet says:

A woman
Not necessary she is pretty
is a poison succulent
....
....

Her charms
in contrast with the soul
are sharper than the edge a razor has
....
She disturbs with her presence
breeds despair with her absence.

("She Disturbs with Her Presence", vol.3, p. 22)

In "How Long could this Relationship Last" in the same volume, he says:

Today
You are standing at a distance.
I do not mind the distance
I have this with so many
I consider my own...

The images of a cottage and a castle for a woman are new and imbued with rich fantastic meaning; a pilgrimage and a thoroughfare; we feel the refreshing charm of the cottage and the dull depressing monotony of the castle. ("A Castle Just Thrills with its Façade", p. 27). Dr. R.C. Shukla presents the strain and stress and smoothness of this strain and symphony in an interesting manner. This is the working of love and sex in man-woman relationship before marriage, in marriage, beyond marriage in extra-marital charms with a different tune and each poem portrays a new object of desire in a new situation. So each poem has an aura of freshness as love and sex are ever-fresh, even it works as a taboo, and it remains an object of incessant charm and desire. The poet conceals nothing and reveals all with the boldness and dare of a saint of love who never finds it stale or stinking, disgusting or despairing, defiling or degrading but rather indispensable to everyday happiness and cheer and peace, whatever be the mood therein.

I often ask: "Who doesn't want love?" and "Who doesn't want to be loved?" Of course, to love is our birth right but to be loved is the privilege desired by all but enjoyed by few. The physical attraction in physical loveliness and physical brightness, glow and gaiety of looks and gait, cheerful and tremulous conversation, smartness and suppleness in the twists, turns and bends of body, the breezy whispers, melodious moans, stormy sighs, outflow of raging passions; resentment, anger, teasing, tearful or cheerful surrender, dreaming of hugs, kisses and bites, union in loneliness and absence, escapades and inscapes—nothing seems rich in diversity of moods, moments, mysteries, maladies, meandering mazy motions, countless come loving for whom we yearn, in whose love we languish and whose wasting influence we cherish and desire. Shukla has touched upon the grace, glamour and grill of the abundance and opulence in the ivory towers or green bowers or thorny bushes or green lands or thick woods with warm steamy flow of freshening fragrances in gullies, streams, brooks and rivers with the gumption of a veteran. This is the poetry of rich romance, inexhaustible diversity, sizzling and steaming enchanting lyricism most suited to the subject and style.

The poet has convincingly established that the fruition and failure of this generative and creative man-woman relationship solely lies in sex and love, requited and unrequited. There is nothing new in all that is essential in this but it has been unsaid and unexpressed in Indian English Poetry so frankly, so honestly, so faithfully—and seeming to be a live record of personal experiences, if not wholly but largely—before Shukla. His art of poesy is a wonderful gallery wherein image after image, situation after situation, persona after persona, the object of desire are inviting and inciting. Given the situation, we wonder at the prevalence and practice of bigamy, polygamy, biandry and polyandry since man and woman became aware of their biological existence. There is profound truth in what perhaps G. B. Shaw has said that marriage is a legalized prostitution. So it is without marriage and it enjoys the dignity of an institution under various professional labels and banners. Single theme, single conversational style, sumptuous simplicity sung on the orchestra of love and sex, occasionally to the accompaniment of bagpipes by the poet. That is what sustains the symphony of the Aeolian harp electrifying the reader with a new current.

The poet tries to understand a woman in her viles and wiles during provocation and love-making whereas wisdom demands that we should make her feel wanted instead of rationalizing her behaviour in such situations. He reflects on romantic love, love as an aesthetic necessity and observes that "love never begins with spirit and, contrary to prevalent practice, never ends at the flesh."(Prefatory Note to Vol.1). Chastity has no relation with love, the poet asserts:

Chastity is not the name of love
Nor commiseration, nor benevolence
It demands food for its need
Food for the eyes
Food for the soul.

("Chastity is not the name of Love", Vol.1, p. 17)

He also claims that sexual cohabitation is not even physical. When it is season, clouds may not rain and simply thunder and roam like pilgrims in the sky; the peacocks also dance looking towards the sky; two grown up leaves touching and bending amorously over each other; the pigeons playing with their beaks and the two penguins bathing and then dancing and chirping. So, says Shukla:

Sex is a proclivity, a symptom
An expression of mood, of intent
It is a prologue to the epic of love
Not exclusively the deed
Which is pure need.

("Sex is not cohabitation alone", p. 18)

Shukla should have used Invocation here, not prologue. He thinks of woman as a fertile field and lauds her functional signification in filling her man's life with bliss and blessing—as caretaker of life yielding hope and consoling her broken and fallen man and endures sustenance while feeding him with the fragrances of her flesh and quintessential honey. ("Woman is a field fertile", p. 24). We are reminded of great British poets like Elizabethan Song writers, Spenser, Donne, Shelley, Keats, Browning and the Pre-Raphaelites who create unending delight in their sensuousness. Love poets are lovers too; successful, failed or defeated, doesn't matter. The poet also thinks of love as an illusion blinking from heaven, a man's obsession for his woman and the poor man loses his sense of judgment and is trapped. Man-woman relationship is unusual as that of glass and stone. Shukla doles out message of lasting wisdom to lovers for their success and fuller realization saying that it is man's manliness she desires and longs to be won and defeated and yearns to reveal her secret fragrances and fruits and honey-pot to her manly man. She doesn't like to and cannot wait and:

> She sacrifices her perfumes
> At the altar of love
> And invites the man to cross over
> Through her gate...
> ("The Woman does not like one who waits", p. 29)

This is a poem of deep and subtle psychological insight into the sexual surrender of woman. The poet maintains and sustains the dramatic beauty of sensuality in not suggestive but provocative manner.

A woman's love is an invasion as she her silence and glance cast a magnetic spell on man and she throws herself in the romancer's ground to gauge herself and her capability, her weapons, to bruise and wound the prey who may turn a recluse. ("A woman's love is an invasion", p. 34) The poet feels that it is not possible to say anything with finality about a woman as she remains undefined and indefinable in her relations. She should be treated as a woman only:

> No final word can be uttered about her
> She is intricate like fate
> Knotty, enigmatic
> She is a woman
> Nothing less, nothing more
> An empty basket
> A wholesome store.
> ("No final word can be uttered about her", p. 37)

So infidelity is new morality, a virtue to be valued, and loyalty in love is a liability, according to Shukla. Here is Hamlet's echo:

> Frailty, thy name is woman!
> (Hamlet in Shakespeare's *Hamlet*, L145, Act I, Sc 2)

It may be difficult to say whether woman is frail or she is the frailty of man or man is frail for her. And:

> Thus conscience does make cowards of us all.
> (Shakespeare's *Hamlet*, L 83, Act III, Sc 1)

Rosalind says in Shakespeare's philosophical romance and the brightest comic bliss *As You Like It* that both men and women are uncertain, of course in love and loyalty but not in sex. Her observation there sums up this persistent consistency:

> Men are April when they woo, December when they wed.
> Maids are May when they are maids, but the sky changes
> when they are wives.
>
> (Rosalind in *As You Like It*, L139-41, Act IV, Sc 1)

The song of Balthasar in Shakespeare's *Much Ado About Nothing* comes as a great solace to women who always distrust men for their loyalty and faithfulness *(perhaps to conceal their own infidelity)*. He sings:

> Sigh no more, ladies, sigh no more,
> Men were deceivers ever;
> One foot in sea and one on shore,
> To one thing constant never.
>
> (Balthasar in *Much Ado About Nothing*, L 57-60, Act
> II,Sc.3)

The vision of romantic love as viewed by Dr. Shukla is also loaded with diversity but he has best presented it as an illusion in which no wise man or woman will indulge. In the poem "Romantic love is not different from an illusion", the poet regards it as deceptive relationship; adulterous love is merely a passion, it is dreamy; it is born of imbalanced thinking. Such a relationship painted with the façade of love is empty, bogus; it is like the majestic fort of the king, mutilated and dilapidated, crumbled and deserted inhabited only by the ghosts. The promises made therein are a willful and blatant transgression of the "boundaries of prudence", hence tormenting and ruinous. Even the great holy scriptures forbid such a venture;

> Who has the courage to renounce religion
> For the sake of love?
> ("Romantic love is not different from an illusion", p.76)

It is senseless love, restless love, rootless love, fatuous love, idiotic love, imbecile love. This is the message of sagacity given with a stern warning to avoid such love and follow the saner course only and be happy! That is why "The desire to come to your dwelling is dead", (p. 87). It is not possible to love without a true spirit:

> Can a man love two women at a time?
> Can a woman
> Repeat the same?
> ....
> ....
> Loyalty is a value very high
> But if loyalties are not allowed to clash
> ....
> Unsanctioned relationship
> The very thought is profane...
> ("The necessity of Spirit is great", p. 95)

Obviously, love enjoys social and moral, and hence, legal and religious sanction. Without it, it is vulgar and profane. Here the poet emphasizes the value of self-restraint and purity. He says:

> It is really exotic
> An enlightened man remains engrossed
> In one woman for the whole of his life.
> ("Romance is not bigger than life", p. 111)

Shukla expects a woman also to be stable, virtuous, truthful, fair, honest, modest, innocent, soft in speech, tender in dealings so that love is not debased and sex doesn't become obscene, vulgar and profane. In many of the poems, he has reflected on this aspect of man-woman relationship as it is not a one-way affair ot traffic. In fact, it is a woman whose suggestions, provocations, innuendoes, ogles, slanting and secret looks, advances etc which elicit initially a fearful response which turns out to be a bold affair later. In his Foreword to the second Volume of *The Parrot Shrieks*, Shukla writes:

> Without any bias or prejudice, my experiences and observations, coupled with my readings have led me to the conclusion that a woman is a great riddle ever to be really understood by a man howsoever enlightened he may claim himself to be.

The poet says:

Women, most of them,
Belong to the fox
While men are obsequious, greedy dogs
Wagging their tails
To the hope of a bone.
("Woman's greatest amulet is her forbearance", p. 46)

I met a woman
As devious as a fox
She regularly prayed, Visited shrines
Welcomed holy men
And also hunted unholy for her lust.
("I met a woman", p. 114)

The poet tells us about an obstinate revengeful woman in a poem with the same title and warns:

Such a woman is dreadful
Her invitations fraught with dangers
Her smiles snares
With an object prolonged.

"Who can surpass woman?" is another assertion of the poet in this regard and he substantiates his point with the example of how Vikramaditya's voluptuous brother, King Bharthari, was duped by Anangsena until Rooplekha enlightened the indulgent man—
"And Anangsena proved to be shoddy before a strumpet." So:

Who can surpass woman
In presenting spurious emotions as genuine? (p. 116)

Dr. Shukla sketches a starved woman in naked images:

The woman staring at you is starved.
She is hungry between her legs
And knows
You can give her something
She requires.
She knows your quality
To kindle, to inflame
Then to cool.
("The woman starved", p. 118)

The poet essentializes the beauty of man-woman relationship when he thinks that modesty in a woman and credibility in a man; that is the true beauty of a woman and that is the real strength of a man like the fragrance of flowers. He questions:

What is a woman without modesty
A man without credibility
And a flower without fragrance?
....
....
Fragrant flowers are dear to gods
Modest women testimonials with their husbands
And credible men
Assets to themselves.

("What is a woman without modesty?", p. 117)

Shukla has not only explained and explored the existing levels and directions of man-woman relationship but has made spontaneous and strenuous effort, in all honesty and earnestness, to dig out the unexplored and unknown layers and depths. No other poet in Indian English Poetry, not even Ramanujan, Kamal Das or Imtiaz Dharker or Dr. Rita Malhotra, and very few in British and American Poetry have done so much with such candour, and even nakedness. In "Commerce", Shukla boldly exposes the hypocrisy of the people who protect under the umbrella of trade their impure adulterated emotions; he knows that not only men but women also are actively engaged in trading sex, we call flesh trade, and it is flourishing under different banners at different levels. This is Women's Lib Movement! It was perhaps Henry James who observed that women are the greatest tyrants over women. People with seeing eyes and feeling hearts also see this going on unabashedly though they may not have the voice to protest to rectify the inhuman wrongs being perpetrated. "Commerce" is a poem of great insight into the movement of man-woman relationship on the tracks leading in different directions for the benefit of one for the other unmindful of the social and moral cost/s it entails. Perhaps this is the most cost-effective as it creates smooth and soothing harvest of relationships and life goes on!

The poet says:

There are traders
Who purchase legs
Guarantee satisfaction
And sell moral lectures given by priests.

I have seen markets
And found women
Marketing cohabitations.
....
....
There are women
Not interested in husbands
They love only nights
And enter into contracts
That naturally expire.

("Commerce", p. 35)

Sensual delight in sexual charm and fascination often leads to sexual desire and its initial continuity with frequency quintessentializes man-woman relationship in the evolutionary process of life the certainty of which is felt in its eternity. However, man's areas of interests are wide and diverse and he is born or lives/loves to work in consonance and harmony with this diversity. This distribution of man's daily load saddens a woman and she reconciles with her escape into arms and embraces of others which is by way of adage described as her infidelity. If man can't stick or confine, why should a woman? Shukla's vision of man may have a deeper touch of sanctity, nobility and transcendental quest for the unknown but betraying a woman's trust/ love, her primary need to be wanted, desired and loved, for this quest must not result in unhealthy practices in the working of this relation with enduring grace and dignity. The poet says:

I cannot sacrifice my duties
They are larger than love
Their boundaries infinite
....
....
All women are islands
And so are you
But an island can only attract
It can never tame a man

Built for things nobler.
....
Let me look beyond you, beyond myself.
....
....
I am in love with jungles, deserts
That symbolize mysteries
Although I take care
My distribution otherwise
Does not make you sad.

("All women are islands", p. 32)

The dilemma of the poet is well-expressed in "I coerce myself", "Those who love are guilty of a sin", "Something within me warns", "But you pestered my peace", "But this again was an illusion", "If my soul craves for you" as the thorn in the flesh is running through veins and the uneasy mind seeks release and relief. His yearning and languishing can be fully discerned in his craving:

If my soul craves for you
And the intimation reaches you in time
The duration of communication
Can offer us 'Anand'
Nothing on this earth can.

("If my soul craves for you", p. 89)

And:

I seek you because I am alone
Because I am incomplete
And you alone can assure
My loneliness can be cured
And my pathetic blanks be stocked.

("I run only because there is a distance", p. 85)

Sometimes the irony is that when a man loves a woman for something inexplainable, she feels puffed up and begins to jeer at love; the poets feels that constancy in relationship is an embellishment. So the poet says:

Relationship springing from within
Is necessity of the soul

But spontaneity alone is not sufficient for its life
Unless honesty is our guide...

("We befriend people just for a change", p. 53)

Finally, we can say that Dr. Shukla has attempted to define the indefinable, love and its nature; the more he has scratches the skin and the head and the heart, the more rashes have appeared effacing and defacing the fair fair, the sublime sublime; the Light of lights, the glow Divine, wrought with human mind—so becoming a thorn in the flesh becoming before and leaving behind "A burning forehead and a parching tongue" (Keats's *Ode on a Grecian Urn*). In the Foreword to the Second Volume of *The Parrot Shrieks*, the poet observes:

> As a matter of fact, the man-woman relationship includes the entire drama of human life, its sweetness, its bitterness, its joys and its despairs. Since woman is the most significant symbolic form of 'Maya', the man who is in serious relationship with her ultimately lives in the world, enjoys it, but is prepared to renounce it too. *Countless men have renounced and countless may do but no woman has ever done so.*
>
> (These *italics* are mine).

Rudyard Kipling says in his poem, "The Female of the Species is More Deadly than the Male", and intellectualizes the issue. Innumerable, gods and goddesses, saints and sages, dukes and duchesses, kings and queens, princes and princesses in all mythologies, literatures, history, folk literatures, Kissa Kavya, etc., have been stung or bitten by Lord Love or hit, wounded and bruised by the piercing arrows of the Cupid or Venus throughout. What wonder if the ordinary mortals in the daily coarse course fall a prey irresistibly to this Lord of Thorns and fall because they do not know how to rise. Shukla has abundantly elaborated these ordinary mortals. He is delighted and spreads infectious gusto and rumbustious ecstasy for the thorn in the flesh to harmonize and soothe man-woman relationship and liberate it from the disturbing, debasing, perplexing and nauseating irritants but not those that sweeten this relationship. There is no self-condemnatory mood and self-torturing guilt anywhere in all moods and moments, passions, panting puffs though the parrot keeps shrieking:

The parrot shrieks
The parrot cries
....
....
The parrot is a thing of entertainment for the dame
An illustration of her skill
Of her capability to tame
And keep him on crumbs.

("The Parrot Shrieks", p. 59)

The world would not have been as we see it, had there been no thorn and the world will go with this thorn! The poet's philosophy of love is best expressed in excellent lyrical beauty in *Love is not a lamb* wherein he sings of the transcending virtue of love not a lamb, not a tiger, not a snake, not a cat but it is indefinable, illusive, abstract, trustworthy and so real:

"Always submissive
Always shy."
He further says:
"Love is half of life
....
....
Love is an ambition to grow
It is a child yearning for its mother
....
An answer
To all the troublesome questions of life."

("Love is not a lamb", p. 38)

I shall conclude with a story of a man-woman race narrated by Master Aristophanes during the usual lively, enlightening, philosophical, metaphysical and moral discussion on love at a routine gathering of the Greek Masters. In his regaling wit, the comedy master said that God had created man-woman race in this world of ours. This race was so powerful that they decided to launch a spirited aggression on gods to recapture heaven. Gods smelt a rat and learnt about the invasion. The poor gods were so scared that they separated the man-woman race to save heavens as their habitat. Since then, men and women have been yearning and languishing to be united!

Works Cited

Alexander, Peter, (ed.), *Shakespeare Complete Works,* ELBS and Collins, London, 1965.

Lawrence, D.H., *Poems,* Volume 1, with Introduction by V. de. S. Pinto, William Heinemann Ltd. 1964.

Praz, Mario, *The Romantic Agony,* Oxford University Press, London, 1970.

Shukla, R.C., *The Parrot Shrieks, Three Volumes* (1-3), A Writers Workshop (as Redbird Book, HB & FB), Kolkata, 2003, 2005, 2008.

Young, Wayland, Eros Denied, Corgi Books, London, 1964.

Thomas & Thomas, HL and DL, *Living Biographies of Great Philosophers,* Bharati Vidya Bhawan, Bombay.

Perspectives, Prospectives and Problems of Teaching Communication Skills (with Special Focus on Engg. & Tech. Students)

I am reminded of *"English Words"*, a glowing tribute to the mellifluousness, beauty, force and impact of English language by Vinayak Krishna Gokak. In this immensely profound and passionate poem, the bureaucrat-poet Gokak has sung about the movement, mobility, and dynamism of English language that has revolutionized the basic structure and fabric of life in india. This language of the angels has shaped up our daily speech, daily intercourse at all levels and has set in an uncontrollable and overwhelming deluge of opportunities and openings, and nothing here remains untouched by its magic wand. This poem of Gokak is worthy of being quoted wholly but we shall quote some indispensably significant lines:

> "Speech that come like leech-craft
> And killed us almost, bleeding us white!
> You bleached our souls soiled with impurities,
> You bathed our hearts amid tempestuous seas
> Of a purer, drear, delight.
>
> O tongues of fire! You come devouring
> Forests of nightshade....
> ....
>
> O winged seeds! You crossed the furrowed seas
> To nestle in the warm and silent earth,
> Like a golden swarm of fireflies you come
> ....

O winging words! Like homing bees you borrow
Grown murmurous, the honey of delight
....
Fathomless words, with Indo-Aryan blood
Tingling in your veins,
The spoils of ages, global merchandise
Mingling in your strains!
You pose the cosmic riddle.
....

Even a casual reading of the whole poem shall not only acquaint us with English of England but convince us about the emergence and use of Indian English. The point is that the flow of English into every vein of life in India started with such a loving spontaneity that it has gone unchecked and we are completely overpowered by it in speech and writing, though the teaching and learning process is largely outdated. Our academic, social, professional, and commercial requirements demand immediate updating of the infrastructure of teaching and learning English to ensure strong communication skills to infuse spirited inputs of success in life's venture.

With marketing and aggressive marketing holding a firm grip on academia and industry, the teaching of Communication Skills(CS) has assumed greater significance, though the inputs and outputs are incompatible changing the very structure of written and spoken English; and even the teaching methodologies. With newer marketing strategies emerging in the global market and businesses having profound diversity, it is increasingly felt in both academia and industry that communication skills of all those engaged and involved in this enterprise and venture, whatever be their level of responsibility, must be strong enough to achieve the desired and declared results and fulfill targets. In this entire strenuous process and exercise, inside and outside the prescribed compulsions and obligations, the teaching and training of communication skills as a subject, meant to determine the future success of the prospective professionals and technocrats, have come to face bigger challenges in their spoken, written and listening skills, though reading skills cultivated through motivation and reading habits at the initial stages are of immense significance as they profoundly contribute to the thought-process without which C.S in any form can't be practised. Reading of social, psychological, literary, scientific and technical etc, material in full comprehensiveness is a primary input in the class room and away from there, especially for those joining engineering and technical courses.

What toughens the task further is the draught conditions in the faculty in a very large majority of cases. With the equally diverse background of the learners accompanied by their lackadaisical approach, the teachers of Communication Skills, almost all from their mindset and commitments in the teaching of literature and language. from the prescribed anthologies with a number of repetitions at the senior secondary and undergraduate level, find it quite and completely different, though not disappointing. Secondly, the purpose of teaching is confined to job-seeking and job-security. Such teachers, with a sense of fulfilment, envious and otherwise, are overcome with a feeling of redundancy in certain respects also in the given situation where Communication Skills teaching occupies an almost negligible status in the general scheme of things in the engineering and technical courses and colleges. The personal, social, economic and professional needs of the learners of C.S. in this atmosphere do not get any stimulus to the level of requisite satisfaction. That is why, crash programmes for PDP and inter-personal skills at a later stage prove of little substance. The revolutionized and globalized business scenario find a little breathing space in the existing syllabus-content and spirit in such institutions, although this provision and facility are non-existent in the institutions teaching humanities and sciences and job-oriented courses, notwithstanding the teaching and learning of English for a variety of reasons and purposes in everyday life for secretarial practice, broadcasting and telecasting, commercial arts, journalism and mass communication, hospitality management, fashion technology, pharmacy and other such allied purposes. The syllabus is also designed keeping in view the purpose of teaching and learning.

Obviously, the yawning gap between the rising expectations and falling fulfilments poses a tough challenge more to the teachers than to anybody else. This further aggravates the situation for all when a large number of unscrupulous persons and personalities make easy and fast buck by starting teaching and learning and spoken English business everywhere to cash in on the mass craze for gaining envious status. We all know that English is a status language, the status which no other subject or language enjoys in these splendid times of fashion, pharmacy, engineering, technology, banking, hospitality, tourism and travel, employment as personal secretaries and receptionists, businesses and what not—and all related to marketing where the total success and upward mobility depend only on the competence in Communication Skills. It matters a least whether your professional knowledge and performance therein have been and are respectable. Dr. Nandini Sahu says:

> The role of English language changed in the post-independent period as a means of social and cultural organizer. Still a majority of English teachers continue to work in isolation till date without realizing the diverse phenomenal qualitative and quantitative growth of the language. In a state of academic confusion and dismay in the last five decades, they have been shifting the language teaching approaches and course contents designing the syllabi in different ways either imported or imposed on them. At present, the second language strategies are being shifted to structural English and communicative English, separating language teaching from literature, splitting the English classics unnaturally, reducing literature and language to objective by comprehension in the name of so-called 'skills'... The students join English as well as Spoken English courses for varied purposes—to enhance their social status, for better mobility, to prepare for competitive examinations, for dynamism in the technical world, and a very few to enter the world of literary sensibility, to study English literature as the core subject. With a view to reaching out to the different parts of the world and becoming global, new English has developed a variety of forms, each one correct within its own context, classified as national, regional, social, occupational which is now termed as ESP, English for Specific Purpose.
>
> *(Introduction to Post-Modernist Delegation to English Language Teaching, P.P. xxx-xxxi, Authorspress, New Delhi, 2005.)*

English, undoubtedly, and by common consent, has become the *lingua franca*. It would be more appropriate to say that *English is a Language For All Practical Purposes.* And who can deny that? All people, anywhere and everywhere, irrespective of their humble or high, social, economic, educational or professional status in rural or semi-urban or urban or cosmopolitan areas, use hundreds of words from English language in their daily conversation, consciously or unconsciously, as if these words belonged to their own mother tongue or as if they were the native speakers of English language and also in their own local or natural accent. For example: fridge, cooler, air-condition, mobile, phone, inspector, cooperative society, railway station, driver, conductor, hotel, college, school, course, university, police, palace, marriage palace, mall, mall road, park, ceremony, coolie, cinema, building, airport, flight, booking, travel agent, passport, taxi, tax, subsidy, bank, loan, corruption, post office, guard, security, function, bag, pen, master, computer, management, machine, combine, chain, gun, revolver, bread, butter, juice, master, headmaster, principal, teacher, engineer, doctor, operation, heart attack, cancer, tension, hospital, accident, cut, power-cut, club, function, singer, film, actor, hero, heroine, director, direct, contest, photographer, video-movie, audio-video, courier, service, pen, marker, pencil, copy, photocopy, beauty parlor, handbag, purse, boutique, cocktail, affidavit, agreement, account, balance, C.A. A/C Payee Cheque, Crossed Postal Order, President, M.D., M.L.A., M.P., member, D.C., S.S.P., Speaker, public, cycle, scooter, car (even the names of the brands), bus, denting and painting, repair, workshop, studio, navy, Air Force, uniform, elections, votes, badmash; even the order for non-veg. items in a restaurant or hotel like: chilly-chicken, butter-chicken, roasted chicken, cream-chicken, leg-piece, fish fried, fish-roasted, fish curry, meat, drinks, etc are placed in English, may be eaten in Panjabi or Hindi.

Then there is the frequent use of compounds-one Hindi and one English word: Dhamaka-sale; Lathi-charge; Double-roti; Kathi-roll; Namkeen-biscuit; Zabardast-accident, etc.

The other day, I was surprised to read in Punjabi: *Linement* for alignment and wheel-balance at an auto repair shop.

The list may not conclude. This is an indispensable part of the daily vocabulary of a large mass of educated and uneducated mass. And there are more than 30,000 words from Hindustani incorporated in the main *Oxford Dictionary*. The Bank of English is working day and night at all public places—airports, malls, theatres and cinema houses, hotels and restaurants, etc. and getting new usages for incorporation into English. With such lavish facilities and conveniences, does it not surprise or stun us to think what obstructs our learning and cultivating our communication skills?

In this age of hybridization, it has not been possible for language for communication purposes in speech and marketing to remain immune. Obviously, educated, half-educated or even uneducated classes feel more comfortable while communicating with others in private or public at both conscious and unconscious levels. It happens mostly when they don't find proper equivalents in their own language and English words come handy and very easy to speak. Even language teachers, especially English teachers, are also great defaulters; teachers of other disciplines take pride in absolving themselves of this serious shortcoming. The other day, I read this marketing slogan at a petrol station:

Saal Bhar Free Fuel Offer.

And at a car repair workshop, this was in Punjabi:

ithe caran di reapir ate denting painting da kam tassalibaksh kita janda hai (here car repairs and the job of denting and painting is done satisfactorily.)

Even the government buildings declare:

"Nagar Council", "Daftar D.C.", "Daftar Senior Police Kaptan" " Civil Courts", "District and Sessions Courts", "Press Club", etc.

I heard an officer saying:

Maine file par noting de di hai (I have given my noting on the file).

This interesting caption was read at the rear of the car

Gabhru on hunt.

This unique phenomena prevail among all classes of people—general public, students, professionals, officials, business or executive class. From where did they learn this art of hybrid communication is difficult to say or analyze. This is the tremendous impact of the astonishing developments in science, technology, computers and IT, means of communication, etc., on the structure of written and spoken English. It has become a fashion also and, perhaps, it has strengthened the communicative competence and performance of all these classes!

But what has wondered me more is the depressing environment for learning language, communication and humanities in the speedily coming up of engineering and technical colleges and institutes in the rural and semi-urban areas. Learning process of Communication Skills in the polytechnics and polytechnic colleges is still more negligible and even deplorable. May be such openings have resulted from the general policy of economic liberalization for achieving the fast-track social, economic, educational development, especially in the rural and backward areas of the country. With all the infrastructure, the learning and teaching of Communication Skills as a subject of course obligation and language have been suffering from cardiac arrest.

All engineering and technical courses are devoid of the teaching of Humanities. My serious and honest observation there has been that even the faculty and, in some cases, Principals/Directors need be given lessons, training and tests, at least twice a month, in Language and Humanities for it is my strong conviction that without interest and reasonable competence in these areas, they can't do justice to their professional responsibilities. It has been shocking to find that they are, almost all, completely ignorant, and even disinterested, in raising the level of their awareness about significant historical, economic, political events and affairs. I remember that my Economics, Political Science, Philosophy, Chemistry, Physics, Maths, and even Hindi teachers were remarkably gifted in their vast range of knowledge and command over the Communication Skills. My Professors of English, Economics and Political Science could discuss anything under the sun because of their scholarship and their students proved their worth and enviable competence in high and very high positions. *This is the Miracle of Communication*

Skills finely clubbed with General Studies! And there was no teaching of CS in those days!

Given such a wealth of words from a *phoren language* we use in our everyday personal, social and professional life, extremely low level of communicative competence and general awareness, we need urgently to have a re-look at the learning and teaching process of CS, of course, English. It is well-known and understood that without communicative competence, the performance of personality remains low; in today's situation, it is largely miserably low. Unless or until some meaningful inputs are provided in all earnestness, we may not ensure a reasonable and acceptable level of communicative competence. It has been painful to observe that the prescribed syllabus of Communication Skills in the technical universities is not only deficient but also irrational and needs immediate overhauling to cater to the professional requirements.

Although there has been a considerable theoretical emphasis and focus on Reading Skills, Speaking Skills, Listening Skills and Writing Skills, negligible effort is made to make all these skills of any practical use. The background of a very vast number of students and their foundations and interest in the language/s, of course, Communication Skills, is pitiable, if not deplorable. The award system and the internal assessment are intolerably faulty. Even the teachers engaged in the subject or programme remain lax for reasons, personal and professional.

At the M.B.A. level also in these institutions, there are no useful parameters to improve their Communication Skills, executive or otherwise. These senior-level students have been seen to be low, if not miserably low, in their level of awareness of the pre-requisites of their tolerable success in future, although these students have diverse academic backgrounds. It further adds to the woes of the learners and teachers when they realize the fast increasing importance of these skills in determining their rate and level of success in the prospective managerial and professional responsibilities. Now when the MNC are widely spreading their net, the learning of other languages like Italian, French, Spanish, German, Chinese, Japanese, etc., is also becoming essential in undertaking joint and collaborative ventures.

This may seem far-off presently in the fast developing rural and semi-urban academic environment. It needs a very serious and immediate look at the prevailing situation in the teaching of Communication Skills, with all the constraints of the workload of other subjects and the general environment. Spending three–four hours in different labs and workshops daily is more or less monotonous and killing and this load may be reasonably reduced to accommodate larger and long-term interests. Some specially compiled anthologies to suit the requirements of English for Specific Purpose with necessary added notes and tips for guided creative writing may be prescribed initially. Then the students be acquainted with the other components of CS. In the final year of their chosen course, a tentative list of great books can be prescribed for independent studies for detailed discussion by the teachers directing the students to write their own impressions and observations about what they understood and felt. This will be a big boost to their CS and partly to their personality development preparing them to readily face the interviews. This will further cure many maladies that downplay their hidden potential. The teaching of CS in these colleges and institutions must enjoy respectable status; the Department of Languages and Humanities be created there as it exists in the NITs and IITs so that the credentials of their students also enjoy their own prestige.

Works Cited

Sahu, Nandini, *Post–Modernist Delegation to English Language Teaching: The Quixotic Deluge*; Authorpress, New Delhi, 2005.

Rizvi, M. Ashraf, *Effective Technical Communication*, Tata Mc Graw–Hill Publishing Company Ltd. New Delhi, 2009.

Gokak, Vinayak Krishna (ed.), *Rhe Golden Treasury of Indo–Anglian Poetry*, Sahitya Academy, New Delhi, 1989.

———————————————15————————————
Aesthetics of Indian Poetics:
A Brief Exposition

(This essay has no claim or pretension to a scholarly or insightful understanding of these terms of Indian Poetics. The sole purpose of this exposition is to simply acquaint the advanced level students of English Language and Literature presuming that the first degree students of Hindi or Sanskrit Literature are well-acquainted with them.)

The study of Indian Poetics is becoming increasingly significant now mainly with the introduction of a complete paper on Indian Writing in English at the postgraduate level in Indian and foreign universities. It has become important also in view of the comparative literary and critical studies. We see that there has emerged a serious and profound interest in the studies of Indian Writing in English because of the newly-acquired pride in our national consciousness and identity. So the scholarship must explore its literary and aesthetic strength, meaning and beauty to establish its status before Western Criticism. It is germane to suggest here that the study of Indian Poetics has added new insight and depths to literary studies. Why so? It shall be clear when we understand how it has an upper cutting edge above the dominating influences.

The terminology of Indian Poetics or Sanskrit Poetics has richness and variety, unparalleled in any other literature. These terms have physical and philosophical, metaphysical and psychological, biological and spiritual with their own unlimited contentual and contextual significance. The knowledge and understanding of some of these specifically and definitely expands our interest and enhances our instruction and delight.

Rasa, dhvani, alankar, vakrokati, riti and *auchitya* make an intellectually illuminating and aesthetically fascinating experience. On the whole, it is an abundantly rewarding exercise. We solemnly realize that these terms are quintessential not only to the study of poetry and drama but also to the ethics and aesthetics of literature which, perhaps, we don't have anywhere else. *It may seem to be absolutism but it is very appropriate to say that Indian Poetics makes us see what actually makes a poem truly poetic.*

Here we learn that words and meaning are the body; *rasa,* the basic element or essence of poetry, is the soul; *dhvani,* the inner element, is the heart. In fact, *Rasa—dhvani* together constitute the soul of poetry. We further learn that the essential element of poetry is extraordinary beauty and divine delight. These are the sanctions conferred by the scholars. We shall try to understand this group of Indian Poetics in greater detail to ameliorate our own delight in the studies of literature, especially poetry and drama. This will not only contradict but also belie Plato's contention about poetry.

1. *Rasa*

The quest of Indian Poetics began, in fact, with a profound insight that a work of art is artistic when it evokes the experience of *Rasa.* This 'rasa' is aesthetic state or experience of the reader and is attained through the power of suggestion or that of imagination. Another scholar, Anandavardhan observes that, in the last analysis, the soul of the poem is revealed, realized and cherished by the sensitive student of poetry. This is equally the state of the artist. He cherishes it for its suggestiveness. And this power of suggestion resides in the poem in the same way as beauty (lavanya) in a woman. But this 'rasa' is not found in the parts or any single part because it is the *enlivening principle of the whole.* Thus every good poem which is truly poetic, involves the power of suggestion, and what is suggested. This is the way of judging the greatness of a poem. Hence, 'rasa' is an essential virtue of a poem.

However, 'rasa' has been discussed at length and widely interpreted and explained by the gifted scholars and critics in their own different ways. In the whole body of Vedic Literature, a variety of meanings of 'rasa' is available—liquid, essence, semen, taste, poison, narcotics, alcohol, recitation, listening, performance, meditation, contemplation, action, service, sacrifice, God, etc., today, in general practice, 'rasa' is used as the delight and taste provided by vegetation, medieval sciences for the growth of body, seeing and hearing drama and poetry. It appears as if the application of 'rasa' was confined to vegetation only; then to their taste and then to their use—intoxication and its quality. In art, this intoxication was construed as delight. Slowly, it came to be applied to every kind of delight; so much so that it came to be used for the delight of the soul. If we are to measure the degree of 'rasa', we may say for the increasing degree—joy, happiness, delight, ecstasy, trance, etc. The development of this world can be explained as:

Rasa>vegetation>taste>usefulness>delight>ecstasy>trance.

In the Vedic Literature, all these usages of 'rasa' are available. But 'rasa' was used first of all from the literary angle in Valmiki's Ramayana, clearly in nine forms.

However, the first-ever poetic use of 'rasa' is found in Vatsayana's *Kamasutra,* the art of sexual enjoyment. After that, it is taken in the sense of beauty and aesthetics in the dramaturgy of Bharat. It is not possible to trace the history and tradition of the poetic use of 'rasa' for non-availability of its use in poetics before Bharat. It obviously means the delight provided by poetry. This delight can be divided into three parts in human life:

1. Sensual or voluptuous delight including carnal pleasures;
2. Mental and intellectual delight; and
3. Spiritual/celestial delight or ecstasy of the soul attained through asceticism or meditation, Salvation—the state of trance when the soul is in direct communion with the Supreme—*Paramananda* or *Brahmananda*.

The imaginary/imaginative use of emotions creates mental delight and not the sensual delight. Keats says in *Ode on a Grecian Urn-*

Heard melodies are sweet but those unheard are sweeter.

This delight is higher than the sensual or sexual delight which leaves behind "burning forehead and parched tongue" andis equal to the Supreme Bliss. These forms of 'rasa' have three attributes:

1. Tamas;
2. Sattvik; and
3. Rajas.

In this way, Bharat has accepted the presence of permanent emotion through the medium of poetic beauty as 'rasa'. Abhinavgupta has interpreted it at the psychological level and has accepted poetics or drama as the medium for the delight of the soul. But, after him, the condition of this was accepted as a social sanction, not poetic or dramatic. It deserves a serious consideration whether beauty as the source of 'rasa' is personal or impersonal, subjective or objective.

In this context, it is seen that Indian Poetics and Western Poetics have two different viewpoints. Those who take beauty as objective argue that the charming beauties of nature like the hills and the rills, woods and meadows and the majestic mountains, rocks and sea, and even a beautiful person, easily thrill and delight anybody and everybody. There is no difference of opinion on this point. However, Bharat has regarded social conditions as essential for the proper evaluation of the beauty of the object. Thus healthy person is essentially by all objects of beauty. When Majnu was told that his Laila was dark-complexioned, he told them to look at her through his eyes. There is abundant truth in this proverbs— "Beauty lies not in the object but in the eyes of the beholder." And "Nobody's sweetheart is ugly."

Thus the concept of beauty changes from place to place, person to person. In India, red complexion, big black eyes, jet black curly hair and thin lips are regarde as beauty; in Africa, dark complexion and thick lips; in Europe, golden hair, brown or blue eyes; in China, little feet and blue-brown small eyes are true beauty. So we can say that beauty is subjective as well as objective. Whatever may be our concept, it is a source of 'rasa' and it is perennial source of delight:

A thing of beauty is a joy for ever— Keats in *Endymion*

Lovers have made supreme sacrifices in love and we have innumerable instances in history. Is it not 'rasa'?

The psychologists believe that neither the feeling of joy nor the feeling of sorrow are completely the source of delight. Generally, the permanent emotions are accepted to be nine. So there are *nine rasas* based on these emotions. Although Indian scholars have not analyzed these permanent emotions from the psychological point of view, Mcdougall has fixed the number of these tendencies/propensities of human behaviour as follows. The intimate relation of these basic human propensities with *rasa* can be explained as under:

Basic Human Tendencies	Rasa
1. Renunciation	Poise, calm, peace (*Shanthi*)
2. Defence	Horror, terror (*Bhyanak, Bhyankar*)
3. Invention	Strangeness (*Adhbhuta*)
4. Love and Sex	Beauty (*Shringar*)
5. Association or sociability or clubbability	Pitiful (*Dayaveer*)
6. Rearing and caring of children	*Vatsalya*
7. Self-importance	Heroism (*Veer*)
8. Creativity	Heroism (*Veer*)
9. Devotion to the brave and the great	Devotion (*Bhakti/ Shraddha*)
10. Looking to others for help in crisis/difficulty	Pathos (*Karuna*)
11. Laughing at or jeering at others' follies	Humour (*Hasya*)
12. Struggle against odds/ difficulties	Anger (*Rudrat*)

Thus these are twelve permanent emotions in psychological analysis of human behaviour as determined by the scholars.

According to the dramaturgy of Bharat, there are actually only four main *rasas*—*Shringar* (Beauty), *Raudra* (Anger), *Vir* (Heroism) and *Bibhatsa* (Calm and peace). The other four *rasas*—*Hasya* (Humour), *Karuna* (Pathos), *Adhbhuta* (Strangeness) and *Bhayanak* (Horror)—are born out of these. These four main *rasas* have been further divided in poetics in view of a large variety of tendencies, conditions and situations. All these kinds of *rasas* have their own aesthetic, ethical, spiritual, intellectual and physical delight. The judicious understanding of *rasas* tells us that the rasa provided by poetry or drama or by meditation are the highest forms of rasa in all conditions-literary, social, psychological and religious. *Alankar* (metaphor or conceit), *Riti* (style), *Vakrokti* (expressionism), *Dhavani* (suggestion), *Auchitya* (appropriateness, propriety, justness, befittingness)—are all associated with *rasa*.

In all principles of Poetics, *rasa* is accepted in some or other way. Obviously, *rasa* emerges out of all beauty in whatever form it is that surrounds us. Herein lies the importance and utility of the *Doctrine of Rasa* notwithstanding opposition to it today.

2. *Alankar*: Analogy, Simile, Metaphor, Conceit, etc.

There is no doubt that *Rasa* is the most ancient principle of poetics but the use of the word *Alankarshastra* in the history of poetics reveals the symbolic importance, popularity and oldness of *alankar*. It is used to mean ornamentation, grace, decoration and even in the sense of perfection. So *alankar* has very deep and wide meaning with equally deeper and wider perspectives. That is why we do not have its exact equivalent in Western Poetics or in English language. It is against this background that we have to discuss its meaning.

In simple words, *alankar* means the word or the basis of the word which adds a special decorative, ornamental, significant and graceful meaning to poetry. There has been a subtle, artistic and highly aesthetic use of *alankars* in Sanskrit poetry or so to say, in Hindi poetry also. For instance, a woman uses a number of make-up devices and ornaments to beautify herself and also to look more charming casting a spell on the on-lookers. She may use perfumes, powders, patches, flowers, necklaces, bracelets, ear rings, nose rings or nose-pins, pearls and beads. But a poet says: "A woman blessed with beauty and grace is not a slave to jewels or ornaments." In poetics, *alankars* have been used in such number of ways from time to time.

Bharat's *Natyashastra* alone is the ancient book on poetics available. Prior to him, the evidence of the discussion of *alankars* by Ram Sharma, Meghabin and Rajmitra is there but no documentary evidence is available. However, the credit of establishing *alankar* as the soul of poetics goes to Bhamah. And it is from his discussion that we come to learn about the significant and meaningful use of *alankar* in poetry since ancient times. Subtle and creative uses of *alankars* have always delighted and enlightened us. This usage may be conscious or unconscious. Thus the ancient use of *alankars* has been undoubted. In the *Rigveda,* the oldest written scripture, we have a clear use of *alankars,* metaphors, analogies, similes. Since Vedic times, *alankars* have been subtly and creatively used in Indian languages. The continuous and consistent increase in the number of *alankars,* tendency to lend inner subtle meaning by innovative use of *alankars* amply bear testimony to their popularity and literary strength and beauty and, even magnificence. The scholar, Dandi, has gone to suggest that even today, *alankars* are being used in forms in in different imaginative creations and none has the full competence to describe them completely.

Alankar and the attributes are the forms of aesthetics. Expression alone reveals the subtlety of the word and meaning. while accepting the *guna* as an impartial and independent soul of poetry, Dandi has acknowledged the true importance of *alankars.* Even Udbhat has included the principles of Bhamah in his *Kavyalankar Saar Sangrah* (The Essence of Poetic Metaphors) (*Tr. mine*). he has stressed the satirical use of *alankar* although Vaman advocates Riti, yet he attaches great importance to *alankar* and he opines that *alankar* alone makes poetry creative. Rudrat, undoubtedly, has realized the significance of *alankars* but he has regarded them as ornamental to word and meaning. Even Anandvardhan, Abhinavgupta, Kuntak and Kshemender have also determined the value of *alankars* in poetry in the light of *rasa* and *dhvani,* though they have placed rasa as higher than *alankar* as the soul of the poetry of highest order. Other literary pundits like Mammat, Vidyadhar, Jayadev, Keshavamittar, etc., have also distinguished themselves in the use of *alankars* in poetry in subtle creative ways.

The modern scholars also sharply differ on the position and importance of *alankars* in poetry. According to Ram Chander Shukla, the forms, properties and actions which provide a supreme expression to emotion are alankars. Even Sumitranandan Pant feels that *alankars* are not meant only for the decoration of the speech; they have a multidimensional use for language, speech, music and passions which determines their very character, ethics and convention. However, Dr. Gulabrai has spoken high of *alankars* saying that they are not at all external ornaments to be worn or discarded at will; they are closely associated with the natural zeal of the poet or the author; the perfection of language largely depends on the use of *alankars*. The above discussion shows that no good poetry can be conceives without *alankars* and it is their subtle, tactical, creative use which lends grandeur and high order to poetry. Moreover, *alankars* are the real richness of poetry, Rishi Balmiki's *Ramayana*, Rishi Vyas's *Mahabharata*, Tulsi's *Ramacharitamanas*, *Dohas* of Kabir, Rahim, etc., reveal infinitely the abundantly rich and creative, philosophically and psychologically subtle use of alankars in poetry.

At first, from Bhamah to Vaman, the number of *alankars* was only 52; then from Rudrat to Ruyyak, newly innovated *alankars* were 51 which made the total number 103. after this, from Jayadev to Jagannath, 88 still more *alankars* were created the number swelled to 191 out of which nine are *shabadalankars* and 182 are *arthalankars*. Even Vakrokati is a *shabadalankar*. *Rupak* and *upama* are also a part of *alankar*. We can cite hundreds and thousands of instances to substantiate the points discussed. This has undoubtedly lent a still larger variety and diversity to meanings in Indian Poetics in all languages and strengthened and expanded their scope, subtlety and sanctity. It convinces us without an iota of doubt that alankars are indispensable to the soul and *rasa* of poetry.

3. *Vakrokti* (Expression, Expressionism, Irony)

Indian Poetics refers to *vakrokti* as a specific kind of poetic expression. Bhamah regarded it as a general name for a figure of speech. It is an expression which deviates from the normal one and it is unique to poetry. Dandi, the eminent scholar, divided all kinds of poetic expression into:

a) Those having the striking or deviating expression (*vakrokti*);

b) Those having the natural descriptive expression (*svabhavokti*)

However, Bhoja found a third group called *rasokti* which is an expression embodying the aesthetic state of experience.

Kuntaka considered *vakrokti* to be the distinguishing feature of all poetry. This feature beautifies the theme, and it is revealed in and through the profound manner of expression. All embellishments and the power of suggestion are enhanced and regulated by *vakrokti*. This is a unique manner of expression which differs from the non–poetic manner because it is the product of of the poet's power. Kuntaka denies the title of poetry to a poetry of statement (svabhavokti). It can be poetry only if the statement is expressed in a strikingly unusual way. Such an expression is poetic only when it can evoke a transcendental delight.

Dandin held that *vakrokti* becomes charmingly subtle when it also involves a play on the meanings of words known as *slesha*. This is analogous to Brooke's paradox or Empson's ambiguity.

For Abhinav, *vakrokti* is synonymous with poetic activity. Imagination, evocation of aesthetic experience, behaviour similar to that of a beloved, the imaginative expression—these are to be found only in poetry. Such is the typical Indian attitude. Even the New Critics in English and American Criticism appear to make a figurative device central to all poetry. Thus it is a living personification or embodiment of substance of poetry; it is a subtle use of speech; device of expression, different from a common speech is *vakrokti*.

This term of Indian Poetics is quite popular but is different from its dictionary and grammatical meaning. it gives birth to a poetic genius. It is concerned with the total process of poetic creation—stanza, sentence, meaning, context etc.that is the reason that Kuntak has accepted vakrokti only as the means of poetic composition; in its absence, there can be no poetry, even if *rasa* is there. We may safely conclude that *vakrokti* is far higher than alankar; the miraculous use of words adoring them with the diverse shades of meaning alone forms the essential element of poetry whereas in *vakrokti*, there is the process of poetic creation also. Similarly, *vakrokti* has a wider scope than *riti* and *riti* can be assimilated in *vakrokti*. In *dhvani*, the power of words only is a poetic mean whereas, in *vakrokti*, this is considered supreme.

:. *Auchitya* (**Appropriateness, Justness, Propriety, Befittingness or Even Spontaneity**)

Auchitya is a very significant term in Indian poetics. The dictionary meaning of auchitya is justness, propriety, appropriateness, or for that purpose, spontaneity. This is the accepted lexical meaning and this is currency. It may also mean befittingness. If we understand its application in wider perspectives and in the context of other essentials like *rasa, alankar, vakrokti, riti* and *dhvani*, we come to learn that auchitya means the rational, and even aesthetic, usage of other elements. Also it needs balance. Briefly speaking, it means the proper use of proper means.

Auchitya is basic to *saundarya* (aesthetics). The balanced and rational use of these ingredients alone invests poetics with splendour. Anything in its rightful and deserving place looks and appears beautiful and delightful. Kshemender says rightly that if a beautiful woman does not wear her ornaments in their proper places, she will not only mar her beauty but also look ridiculous. For example, necklace round her waist, her nose-pin in her ears, the anklets on her wrists, etc., will have no *auchitya* anywhere. Even the ornaments will mock in this position. In the same way, to punish the afflicted person or to show bravery to the already suppressed or to pity your enemy will be foolishness and shall never be considered appropriate. Such a person will look ridiculous and deserving of criticism. This shows that *auchitya* alone lends beauty, interest and grace and dignity to these articles and attributes. Its field is not only people but also poetics. It further reveals that auchitya may have emotional or unemotional aspects.

Auchitya is so deep and comprehensive that there can be no tenderness or flow of delight, no significance of dhvani, etc., without it. This is fundamental to all the five principles of poetics. In fact, it is and it determines a code of conduct with its boundless sphere. Its value is undoubted in every form, sphere and situation of life. This is decisive and in itself rational which distinguishes between right and wrong, saint and sinner, ugly and beautiful, just and unjust, true and untrue. It has all the sanctions of law in life. So it has the same supreme importance in literature as it has in life. In dramaturgy also, the stage presentations or enactments or even stage paraphernalia are governed by the infallible principle of *auchitya*. This is equally necessary even in public morality and public behaviour. This alone dignifies delight on firm moral grounds. In fact, it is a rational insight into the appropriateness or propriety of all the elements in poetics.

Although the renowned scholar, Kshemender, has given supreme position to auchitya in poetics, yet we find its mention in ancient poetics also. Great scholars and critics like Bharat, Anandavardhan and Abhinava were already familiar with its importance. However, the basis of its significance lies in its utility and utmost necessity, according to Kshemender. Bharat imparts practical importance to it in dramatics. Bharat has not clearly discussed it but he has indirectly indicated its position. Others like Dandi, Vaman, Yashovarman, Lollat, etc., have also pointed out its significance. The first experimentalist to use auchitya in poetics is Rudrat. In his book, *Kavyalankar* (The Poetic Metaphor), Tr. mine, he has thoroughly discussed, with a critical insight, the meaning, function and utility of *auchitya* with its application to *chhand*, *riti* and *vriti*, *alankar*, rhetoric, community, dynasty, scholarship, finance, country, place, character, etc.

In the Western canons of literature and criticism, *auchitya* has been used with its equivalents—propriety, decorum, appropriateness, adaptation, fitting and grace. These Western scholars have also emphasized its special importance. It is, in fact, the harmonizing principle. Aristotle has stressed the need for the appropriateness in plot, character and language. In his *Rhetoric*, Aristotle says, "The appropriateness of language is one means of giving an air of probability to the case—It is a general result of their considerations that if a tender subject is expressed in harsh language or a harsh subject in tender language, there is a certain loss of persuasiveness." Horace and Dante, Dryden and Coleridge have also emphasized the importance of auchitya in their own way.

Even a poet has to be scrupulously conscious about auchitya while he is engaged in creative poetic process. It is this which determines the relation of *rasa* with other poetic elements. It brings in complete order and balance. Kshemender did a great service to Indian poetics by his serious reflections on *auchitya*. He has observed that it has no opposition to or contradiction with any other principle of poetics. Thus we see that *auchitya* is not a particular doctrine or principle but a highly significant, comprehensive and indispensable ingredient not only of poetics but also of our existence.

5. *Riti*: Tradition, Path, Direction, Guidelight, Style, etc.

Eminent scholars of Indian Poetics have been engaged in serious deliberations about the lexical and figurative and situational meaning of *riti*, its attributes and its position as a doctrine for centuries. They have always differed on certain significant issues pertaining to its meaning, application and usage. The study of the history of Indian Poetics shows that *riti* had been discussed even when it was only the dawn of poetics. Vaman is credited with extolling *riti* as an independent principle of poetics. But many other renowned scholars like Bhamah, Banbhatt, Rajshekhar, Kuntak, Dandi, Bhojraj, Mammt etc. had discussed *riti* in detail and made a good cor.tribution to its development.

Bharat has used propensity/tendency/leaning as a closer but more comprehensive substitute for *riti* in *Natyashastra*. He has brought out distinctive features of propensity on the basis of the living standards and conduct of the people. This has the traces of their nomenclature on the geographical/regional basis. We can understand that Bharat's distinctions are concerned more with the external equipment of drama and less with the fundamental elements of poetics. Bharat has gone into greater details to discuss the other principles of poetics and the very essentials of the doctrine of *riti* include all the attributes and shortcomings of poetics.

It may not be possible for us to find the exact equivalents or synonyms or attributes of *riti* in English as it has been used or coined by its exponents or scholars in Sanskrit or Hindi. However, *riti* with its general and complete meaning is not only tradition but also style. It is distinct or distinguished poetic composition. Words used or clubbed or compounded consciously or unconsciously with diverse shades of meaning emerge as style. The presence of this special attribute lends it uniqueness and Vaman accepts style as the very basis of poetics, its soul, and makes it its supreme element. Thereby develops uniformity, simplicity, melody, lucidity, plainness, alliteration, satire, humour, polish, liberality, embellishment, contemplation, complexity, obscurity, etc. The style may also be personal, intimate, lyrical, ornamental, etc. Some literary masters have divided style into three categories—Attic, Asiatic and Rhodian.

It may also be noted that poetic composition is decorated with analogies, similes, metaphors, conceits—*upma, alankar, vakrokti,* etc.—images of beauty in and around us and symbols, simple, complex and pure with all their appropriateness. This poetic process known as *riti* is creative of beauty which in its totality becomes the soul of poetics and the delight of the poet himself. Otherwise who would enjoy and love reading poetry? This is an indispensable part of true beauty and is an ample justification of this viewpoint. So Vaman was the first to use *riti* for distinct poetic creation. Similarly, Rudrat was the first to relate *rasas* with *ritis*. Thus *riti* is not a class but a doctrine. It may be specially mentioned that *riti* has not been studied from the psychological or ethical point of view in poetics. In the Western Poetics, we have style and it has been defined and discussed quite elaborately and variously by the intellectual luminaries since ages and we needn't discuss it here.

6. *Dhvani:* Suggestion, Suggestiveness

Suggestion or suggestiveness is the nearest equivalent for dhvani in the western literature. It was propounded by a highly renowned scholar, Anandavardhan and supported by Abhinavgupta, Mammat, Kuntak, Lollat, Panditraj Jagannath, etc. The Western scholars believe that the development of words and language occurred simultaneously with the general progress of humanity and economic growth. There are undoubtedly other reasons also but we subscribe largely to the Western view of the origin and evolution of words and their meanings. Today we use a number of foreign phrases in order to enhance the suggestiveness of the words.

However, since *dhvani* enjoys an important place among the principles of Indian Poetics, we learn that the most antique book available on dhvani is Anandvardhan's *Dhvanilok*. There is evidence of the use of *dhvani* prior to him also but no book is extant on it; so the credit of its significance in poetics goes to Anandavardhan only. According to him, *dhvani* is the soul of poetics and it is essential to know and understand its relation with words as a power, as a force, as a potent force. *Dhvani* is the capability of a language to convey or communicate a meaning different from what it seems to be. The scholars of Indian Poetics have pointed out the different categories to explain how *dhvani* works but unfortunately, we don't have the near or appropriate words to elaborate their viewpoint.

We understand it well that there is surface meaning, lexical meaning, implied meaning, connotation, direct meaning, associational meaning, situational meaning, figurative meaning, satirical meaning etc. There are hundreds of commonly known and accepted words with their directly known meanings. We can cite the examples—water, milk, man, woman, lion, teacher, father, mother. God, nature, sky, sun, clouds.. the list is unending and has the clarity of meaning. thje known scholars have different opinions to express on how it happens. There are elusive or labyrinthine or differently or variously suggested meanings when words become analogies, similes, metaphors, symbols—simple, complex and pure. This is an immense and intense source of delight in poetics. That is why there is an intimate relation of *dhvani* with, *rasa, alankar, vakrokti, riti* and *auchitya*. Obviously, dhvani also occupies a significant place in Indian Poetics.

Works Cited

Bisht, Dr., *Jagat Singh: Kavyashastra Ke Siddhant*, Takshshila Parkashan, Delhi, 2002.

Choudhari, Satyadev, *Bhartiya Kavyashastra: Subodh Vivechan*, Alankar Parkashan, New Delhi, 2003.

Choudhary, Tejpal, *Bhartiya Avam Paschatya Kavyashastra Ki Rooprekha*, Vikas Parkashan, Kanpur, 2007.

Gupt, Ganpati Chander, *Bhartiya Avam Paschatya Kavyashastra*, Lok Bharati Parkashan, Allahabad, 2003.

Singh, Bachchan, *Bhartiya Avam Paschatya Kavyashastra Ka Tulnamatak Adhiyan*, Sahitya Academy, Haryana, Chandigarh, 1987.

Verma, Harishchander, *Bhartiya KJavyashastra*, Sahitya Academy, Haryana, Panchkula, 2005.

Verma, Ram Chander, *Bhartiya Kavyashastra*.